THE WAR OF 1812

CHRONICLE OF AMERICA'S WARS

Diana Childress

ℒ LERNER PUBLICATIONS COMPANY

MINNEAPOLIS

CHAPTER PHOTO CAPTIONS

Introduction: British sailors take U.S. seamen from the U.S. ship *Chesapeake*. These men were imprisoned as deserters from the British navy.

Chapter 1: A British press-gang prepares to board a U.S. ship.

Chapter 2: The St. Lawrence River separates eastern Canada from the United States. It is the major water route from the Atlantic Ocean to the Great Lakes area.

Chapter 3: The U.S. ship the *Hornet* captured the British *Resolution* on February 14, 1813. That year the United States began to win some victories on land and at sea.

Chapter 4: The USS *Chesapeake* battled with the HMS *Shannon* just outside Boston Harbor. The last words of the U.S. captain, James Lawrence, "Don't give up the ship!" became the motto of the U.S. Navy.

Chapter 5: General Andrew Jackson addresses the Tennessee militia in 1814 before the battle against the Red Sticks at Horseshoe Bend.

Chapter 6: An old print of the United States Capitol Building shows how it looked in 1812.

Chapter 7: General Andrew Jackson led the U.S. army and militia in the Battle of New Orleans in 1815.

Epilogue: U.S. and British representatives signed the Treaty of Ghent in 1814, ending the War of 1812.

Lerner Publications Company
A division of Lerner Publishing Group
241 First Avenue North
Minneapolis, MN 55401

Website address: www.lernerbooks.com

Library of Congress Cataloging-in-Publication Data

Childress, Diana.
    The War of 1812 / Diana Childress.
      p.   cm. — (Chronicle of America's wars)
    Includes bibliographical references and index.
    Contents: The road to war — Losses on land, victories at sea — The pattern changes — A new front and a victory in the Northwest — The Creek vanquished, the last invasion — The British counterattack — A dramatic end.
    ISBN: 0–8225–0800–1 (lib. bdg. : alk. paper)
    1. United States—History—War of 1812—Juvenile literature. [1. United States—History—War of 1812.] I. Title. II. Series.
    E354.C47 2004
    973.5'2—dc22   2003018805

Manufactured in the United States of America
1 2 3 4 5 6 – JR – 09 08 07 06 05 04

TABLE OF CONTENTS

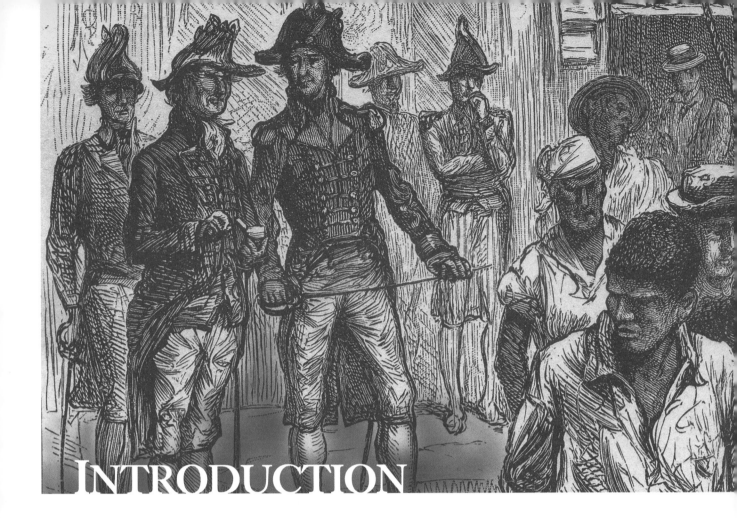

INTRODUCTION

On a bright morning in June 1807, a U.S. warship, the *Chesapeake,* sailed from Hampton Roads, Virginia, on its way to Europe. Supplies for the journey and the baggage of several passengers cluttered the deck. Sick crew members rested in hammocks strung up in the fresh air.

As light winds carried the ship out of Chesapeake Bay and into the Atlantic, a British warship, the *Leopard,* hailed the *Chesapeake.* Calling over a speaking trumpet, the British captain said that he had a dispatch for *Chesapeake* captain James Barron.

The dispatch was an order to allow the British to search the U.S. frigate (smaller warship) for deserters from the British Royal Navy. Captain Barron refused and sent a note back, saying he knew of no deserters aboard the *Chesapeake.*

Fearing the worst, however, Captain Barron ordered the decks cleared for action. Within minutes after receiving Barron's response, the *Leopard* pulled ahead of the *Chesapeake* and fired a warning shot across its bow (front end). The Americans frantically moved passengers and patients below decks and opened the magazines, the place where the gunpowder was stored. Then the *Leopard* fired a broadside—all of the 26 guns facing the *Chesapeake* one after the other in rapid succession. As the iron balls hit the *Chesapeake,* flying wooden splinters sliced the air, wounding many, including Captain Barron.

Before the crew even found their matches, a second broadside hit the *Chesapeake.* A U.S. gunner set off one cannon with a burning coal from the galley stove. But it was too little, too late. Captain Barron ordered the flag lowered in surrender just as a third broadside struck. In the brief, one-sided battle, three Americans were killed and eighteen wounded.

Officers from the *Leopard* boarded the *Chesapeake* and seized four men they claimed were deserters from the Royal Navy. Three were native-born Americans. Only one was British. The United States angrily protested this infringement of U.S. rights. The British later apologized. It was five years, however, before two of the Americans were freed and

returned to the United States—the third died in prison. By then tensions between the two countries over this and other issues had erupted into war.

On June 18, 1812, President James Madison declared war on Great Britain. Although called the War of 1812, it lasted until February 17, 1815. Its battles were fought along the Canadian border, on the Atlantic coast, and at sea.

After the Revolutionary War, U.S. statesman Benjamin Franklin had said, "The War of the Revolution has been won, but the War of Independence is still to be fought." By forcing Britain to recognize the United States as an independent nation, not a former colony ready to serve British global interests, the War of 1812 achieved real independence for the United States. This independence paved the way for the expansion of the United States into a major nation and the world power that it is in modern times.

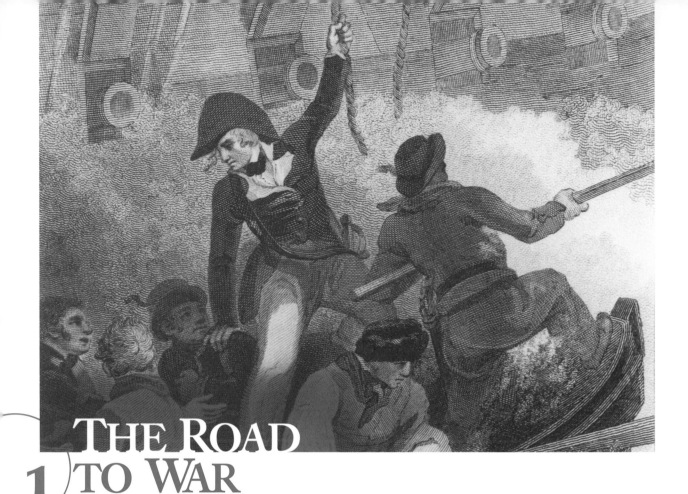

THE ROAD
1 TO WAR

In the early 1800s, the United States was a small but growing country. Since the Revolutionary War, the United States had expanded to 18 states: the original 13 plus Vermont (achieving statehood in 1791), Kentucky (1792), Tennessee (1796), Ohio (1803), and Louisiana (1812). The United States also held the Indiana, Illinois, and Michigan Territories to the northwest, the Mississippi Territory south of Tennessee, and the Missouri Territory, which stretched from the Mississippi River to the Rocky Mountains. It was part of the land President Jefferson had bought from France in 1803 in a deal known as the Louisiana Purchase.

Almost eight million people lived in the United States, mostly along the Atlantic coast and inland rivers. About 90 percent lived on farms and plantations. In the territories, the few forts, trading posts, settlements, and villages of Native Americans were scattered through vast stretches of wilderness and virgin forests.

Surrounding the United States were lands belonging to two European colonial powers, Britain and Spain. Except for a small stretch of the Louisiana coast, all of the land bordering the Gulf of Mexico (including Florida), and all of the land west of the Rocky Mountains and south of Oregon belonged to Spain. Spanish control of its American colonies was being challenged, however, by wars for independence in Mexico and South America.

To the north lay seven British colonies: Lower Canada (the present-day province of Quebec), Upper Canada (the present-day province of Ontario), Newfoundland, Nova Scotia, New Brunswick, Isle St. John (later renamed Prince Edward Island), and Cape Breton Island. Each colony had its own colonial government, which was overseen by a governor-general appointed by Britain. Both the British colonies to the north and Spanish Florida to the south were more thinly populated than the United States.

IMPRESSMENT

The *Chesapeake-Leopard* incident in 1807 was not the first or the last time British ships seized U.S. seamen from U.S. ships. Between 1803 and 1812, about 6,000 U.S. sailors were taken from merchant (trade) and naval ships and forced to serve in the Royal Navy.

Impressment, as this forced service was called, was the Royal Navy's chief means of recruiting men. Britain was at war with Napoleon Bonaparte, the emperor of France and a brilliant general whose armies were conquering Europe. To defend the British Isles, Britain needed a strong navy. But few men volunteered for the Royal Navy because it was known for strict discipline—enforced by frequent whippings—terrible food, and meager pay. Many sailors deserted ship the first chance they got. British warships had press-gangs to carry out the impressment. These gangs roamed ports in Britain and elsewhere in Europe, seizing men and forcing them into the Royal Navy.

U.S. merchant ships offered higher pay and better working conditions than the Royal Navy. U.S. trade grew rapidly during the early 1800s, and U.S. ships, needing trained seamen, hired many British sailors. The British government believed that in the interest of international cooperation, the United States should allow them to reclaim British deserters.

Many deserters from the Royal Navy, however, were U.S. sailors who had been illegally impressed by the British in the first place. The three Americans taken from the *Chesapeake* had been impressed by the British off the coast of Spain. When the British ship they had been forced to serve on pursued French ships into Chesapeake Bay, at the border of Maryland, Delaware, and Virginia, the three took advantage of being near home. They fled the ship in a rowboat, dodging bullets as they rowed and cheering happily when they made it to shore.

French emperor Napoleon Bonaparte

EYEWITNESS QUOTE: IMPRESSMENT

"With much abuse, they hauled me out of my bed, not suffering me to even put on or take anything except my [trousers].

In this miserable condition I was taken on board their ship but did not think to be detained there for . . . seven years. Had I known my destiny that night, I would have instantly committed the horrid crime of self-murder."

—James Durand, U.S. seaman impressed into the British Royal Navy, July 1809

FREE TRADE

The war in Europe also affected U.S. shipping. In 1806 Britain blockaded many northern European ports to prevent France from receiving supplies from overseas. France responded by declaring a blockade on Britain. Ships from the United States and other neutral countries risked attack if they carried goods to or from Britain and France or their colonies.

To solve the problem, President Thomas Jefferson proposed that the United States stop all of its overseas trade. Without U.S. trade, Jefferson argued, Britain would suffer economically and agree to end impressment and the blockades.

In December 1807, the United States passed the Embargo Act, prohibiting almost all trade with foreign nations. The law angered U.S. ship owners, merchants, fishermen, and sailors. One congressman said the embargo was like trying "to cure corns by cutting off the toes." The U.S. government repealed the Embargo Act in 1809 and resorted to other economic sanctions (actions designed to put pressure on a nation that is violating international law), which also failed to solve the problem.

After the embargo was lifted, U.S. merchant ships tried to get around the British and French blockades by carrying two sets of documents, one to make their cargo acceptable to the French and another to make it acceptable to the British. Other captains bribed customs officials. Even so, U.S. ships were seized as often as every two days, according to Secretary of State James Monroe. Between 1807 and 1812, about 900 U.S. merchant ships were captured by France or Britain or their allies. With so many losses of ships and cargoes, and of men to impressments, "Free Trade and Sailor's Rights" became the rallying cry of Americans who opposed Britain's control of the seas.

TROUBLE IN THE NORTHWEST

The United States was also meeting opposition as Americans moved west into new U.S. territories, where they cleared wilderness land for farming. Many Native

In the early 1800s, pioneers began moving west into lands inhabited by Native Americans. Tensions flared as the settlers clashed with the local Native American populations.

In a fierce encounter, Native American warriors fought the troops under William Henry Harrison at the Battle of Tippecanoe in 1811.

Americans who lived there resented the loss of their homes and hunting grounds. Tecumseh, a Shawnee chief, urged native groups to join together to resist American settlement. He and his brother Tenskwatawa, known as "the Prophet," built Prophetstown on the Tippecanoe River, near modern-day Lafayette, Indiana, where they gathered followers.

Other Native American groups, however, were willing to sell land to American settlers. In 1809 several chiefs signed the Treaty of Fort Wayne, selling three million acres in present-day Indiana to the U.S. government—including land where Tecumseh and his warriors hunted.

To protest the treaty, Tecumseh met twice with the governor of Indiana Territory, William Henry Harrison. The chiefs had no right to sell the land, Tecumseh said, because "the Great Spirit intended it as the common property of all the tribes, nor can it be sold without the consent of all." Harrison did not back down. American settlers already outnumbered Native Americans

about four to one in the Great Lakes area.

In the fall of 1811, Tecumseh traveled south to recruit more supporters for his idea of a united Indian nation. While he was away, Governor Harrison marched an army of 970 men along the Wabash River. When he camped near the Tippecanoe River on November 6, Tenskwatawa convinced the warriors in Prophetstown to attack the U.S. troops during the night. Believing the Prophet had magic powers to protect them, 600 to 700 warriors stormed the camp. The army was caught sleeping. Both sides lost many fighting men.

After the battle, Harrison's troops destroyed Prophetstown and discovered a large supply of British weapons. To keep the Native Americans friendly, the British colonial government in Canada had been giving them rifles and other gifts. Many Americans saw the weapons as proof that the British were encouraging Native Americans to attack American settlers.

When Tecumseh returned to find Prophetstown in ruins, he decided to turn to the British for help. In the spring of 1812, Tecumseh and his warriors traveled to Fort Malden in Upper Canada to ally themselves with the British.

THE WAR HAWKS

When the twelfth Congress met in November 1811, war was on everyone's mind. Referring to the impressment of sailors and the seizing of merchant ships, President Madison accused Britain of "tramping on the rights which no independent nation can relinquish." He urged Congress to put the United States "into an armor and an attitude demanded by the crisis."

Madison did not mention war, but many congressmen considered it a "war message." The Speaker of the House, Kentucky congressman Henry Clay, became the spokesman for a pro-war group known as the "War Hawks." Congressmen from southern and western states argued that the United States could put pressure on Britain

by invading Canada. The British colonies to the north seemed like an easy target. Only about 500,000 people of European (mainly British and French) descent lived in Upper and Lower Canada. Many of them were Americans who had moved there because they were attracted by good, inexpensive farmland. Surely, these people would side with the United States, not Britain, in a war.

New Englanders disagreed with the War Hawks. "If you had a field in Georgia," Massachusetts congressman Josiah Quincy noted, "it would be very strange to put up a fence in Massachusetts. And yet, how does this differ from invading Canada, for the purpose of defending our [naval] rights?"

"We cannot contend with Great Britain on the ocean," a congressman from Pennsylvania argued. "Our vessels will only tend to swell the present catalogue of the British navy"—that is, our ships would only be captured and used against the United States, according to the congressman. In the

A Tennesseean Views the War

War fever was especially strong on the western frontier. On March 7, 1812, Major General Andrew Jackson of the Tennessee militia (soldiers called up in an emergency) issued a stirring call for volunteers.

"War is on the point of breaking out between the [U]nited States and the King of [G]reat Britain!" Jackson announced.

"Who are we?" he asked. "For what are we going to fight? Are we the titled Slaves of George III [the British king]? the military conscripts [drafted soldiers] of Napoleon the great? or the frozen peasants of the Russian Czar [ruler]? No—we are the free born sons of [A]merica; the citizens of the only republick now existing in the world; and the only people on earth who possess rights, liberties, and property which the[y] dare call their own."

He promised volunteers that there would be soul-stirring military music and views of such "stupendous works of nature" as Niagara Falls and Montmorency Falls, a 250-foot-tall waterfall near Quebec City.

Tecumseh's Followers

Tecumseh (*right*) became the leader of a confederacy of warriors from many different Native American groups. The Shawnee, Kickapoo, Winnebago, Sac, Wyandot, Menominee, Munsee Delaware, Potawatomi, Ojibwa, Ottawa, and Sioux were among the Native Americans who fought alongside the British in the war against the United States.

end, Congress passed bills increasing the size of the army, defeated a bill to strengthen the navy, and voted for new taxes to pay for the war, if one began. By the spring of 1812, the United States was on the brink of war.

WAR IS DECLARED

On June 1, President Madison sent Congress a message. He detailed Great Britain's disregard for the rights of the United States as an independent country and its contempt for international law on the high seas and on the western frontier. He urged Congress to vote for war. "We behold," he said, "on the side of Great Britain a state of war against the United States, and on the side of the United States a state of peace towards Great Britain."

New Englanders objected to war because they thought the issues could be settled by diplomatic negotiation. They also believed that the southerners were motivated by a desire to grab land from Canada. Voting 79 to 49 in the House of Representatives and 19 to 13 in the Senate, Congress passed the closest vote on any declaration of war in U.S. history. President Madison signed the bill into law on June 18, 1812.

In a highly debated decision, President James Madison (*right*) entered the United States into war for the first time since it had won independence from Great Britain 29 years earlier.

THE HOME FRONT

When war broke out, American reactions depended upon region and political party. (The nation's main parties were the Federalist Party and the Democratic-Republican Party.) This was not surprising given the close vote in Congress. In mainly Federalist New England, Governor Caleb Strong of Massachusetts declared a day of mourning. People fasted and dressed in black. Flags flew at half-mast. Church bells tolled. Together with the governors of Connecticut and Rhode Island, Strong challenged orders to call up the state militia to support the regular army, which was gathering to invade Canada. According to the U.S. Constitution, the governors argued, state militias were supposed to defend states from invasion or rebellion, not wage war on a neighboring country.

Opposition to the war remained strong in New England throughout the war. In December 1814, a convention of New England states was held in Hartford, Connecticut. The idea of withdrawing from the Union (United States) and making a separate peace treaty with Britain was discussed, although voted down.

In northern Vermont and New York, people opposed the war for two reasons. First, they feared being caught in the midst of war. And second, they depended on trade along the water route from Lake Champlain up the Richelieu River to Montreal, Canada. A Plattsburgh, New York, resident complained, "This war . . . has been commenced in folly, directed in weakness, and will end in ruin."

Opponents to the war living in other parts of the country risked the wrath of the pro-war party. In Baltimore, Maryland, when a newspaper dared to criticize the war as "unnecessary" and "inexpedient" (not advisable), an angry mob destroyed the newspaper's offices. When the militia finally put the newspaper staff and their defenders in jail for their protection, the mob broke into the jail, killing one and severely injuring 11 others. No one was arrested for the attacks.

In contrast, volunteers flocked to recruiters in the frontier states of Kentucky, Ohio, and Tennessee. So many men signed on that the army was hard put to supply them all with food, uniforms, weapons, and training.

The war directly affected people living on the northern borders, in western territories, and along the Atlantic coast. The British seized, looted, and burned homes and properties. Many civilians (citizens not serving in the military) lost their lives.

For almost all Americans, the war brought economic hardship. The British blockade of American ports meant that goods once shipped along the coast had to travel by wagon train, which was much slower and more expensive. With the added cost, prices soared. One hundred pounds of sugar that cost $9 in New Orleans, Louisiana, sold for $40 in New York. One hundred pounds of rice cost $3 in Charleston, South Carolina, and $12 in Philadelphia, Pennsylvania. Prices for tea, coffee, and other imported goods kept rising. Prices on U.S. goods dropped at their places of production because it was too costly to ship them to markets. Farmers could not sell their produce, but paid high prices for things they needed.

2 LOSSES ON LAND, VICTORIES AT SEA

For all the years of growing hostility, the United States was not really ready for war. The senior officers in the army had not fought since the Revolution, and most enlisted men (soldiers of low rank) had no military experience at all. But attacking Canada promised to be simple, "a holiday campaign," one congressman predicted.

The main geographic boundary between the eastern United States and Canada is the waterway formed by the St. Lawrence River, Lake Ontario, the Niagara River, and Lake Erie. These lakes and rivers also formed a major natural highway for Canadians, reaching from outposts like Fort Malden at the western end of Lake Erie to Montreal and Quebec City in the east. Forts on both sides defended the waterway, in some cases facing each other across narrow straits. By capturing key forts along this waterway, the Americans hoped to cut off Britain's supply line to Canada.

An Easy Conquest

Many Americans thought conquering Canada would be simple. They assumed that the Americans and French living there would be eager to join the United States. President Jefferson wrote to a friend in early August 1812 that the conquest of Canada would be "a mere matter of marching."

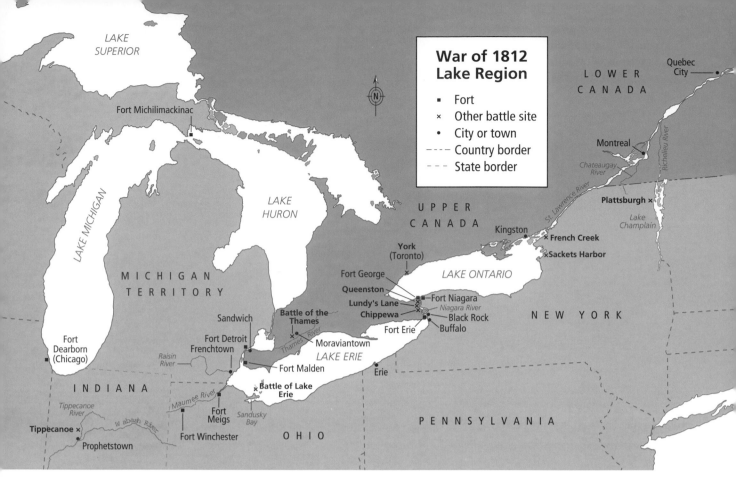

War of 1812 Lake Region map showing forts, battle sites, cities, and borders across the Great Lakes region. Labels include: LAKE SUPERIOR, LAKE MICHIGAN, LAKE HURON, LAKE ONTARIO, LAKE ERIE, MICHIGAN TERRITORY, INDIANA, OHIO, PENNSYLVANIA, NEW YORK, UPPER CANADA, LOWER CANADA, Quebec City, Montreal, Kingston, Plattsburgh, Sackets Harbor, French Creek, York (Toronto), Fort George, Queenston, Lundy's Lane, Chippewa, Fort Niagara, Black Rock, Buffalo, Fort Erie, Erie, Battle of Lake Erie, Battle of the Thames, Moraviantown, Sandwich, Fort Detroit, Frenchtown, Fort Malden, Fort Meigs, Fort Winchester, Fort Dearborn (Chicago), Fort Michilimackinac, Tippecanoe, Prophetstown, Sandusky Bay, Raisin River, Maumee River, Wabash River, Tippecanoe River, Thames River, Niagara River, St. Lawrence River, Chateaugay River, Richelieu River, Lake Champlain.

**War of 1812
Lake Region**

- ■ Fort
- × Other battle site
- • City or town
- --- Country border
- -- State border

President Madison and the War Department planned a threefold attack. In the Northwest, one army would cross the Detroit River into Upper Canada and capture Fort Malden. In western New York State, another army would attack across the Niagara River to capture Forts George and Erie. The third army would advance northward from Lake Champlain and seize Montreal.

The U.S. Navy, with only 17 ships, lagged far behind the 1,000 ships of Britain's Royal Navy. Many U.S. naval officers, however, had seen action in the Mediterranean region during the War with Tripoli from 1801 to 1805. The large numbers of U.S. seamen who had been impressed into the Royal Navy had received excellent training in naval warfare aboard British ships. They were eager to fight for their country and against the nation that had forced them into service.

THE FIRST INVASION

During the spring of 1812, many Ohioans answered the call for men "to fight against perfidious [treacherous] England." By mid-June, General William Hull, a 59-year-old veteran of the Revolutionary War, was ready to set out from Urbana, Ohio, across the wilderness to the Canadian border with an army of 2,000 militia and regular (non-militia) troops. Some soldiers had sewn

General William Hull

signs on their caps that read: CONQUER OR DIE.

Building a road as they went, the army took almost three weeks to reach the U.S. fort at Detroit, about 160 miles from Urbana. The invasion of Canada began July 12, when Hull's army crossed the Detroit River to the town of Sandwich. The British did not contest the landing. Hull assured Canadians, "I come to *protect* you not to *injure* you." About 400 Canadian militiamen joined the Americans. Many others simply went home to harvest their crops.

Hull was having wagons built to carry heavy artillery (large, mounted firearms) to attack the British at Fort Malden 14 miles away, when news arrived that U.S. Fort Michilimackinac in northern Michigan Territory had surrendered to the British and their Sioux, Winnebago, and Menominee allies. Fearing this victory would lead to further raids by Native Americans, Hull sent a warning to Fort Dearborn on Lake Michigan, where the city of Chicago stands in modern times, urging the small garrison (military post) to evacuate.

Hull was also worried about feeding his army. Provisions sent from Ohio needed a military escort. On August 5, when 200 soldiers left Detroit to meet a supply train, they were ambushed and chased back to Detroit by 25 Native Americans led by Tecumseh.

A few days later, Hull received news that British reinforcements had been seen arriving at Fort Malden. For safety, he pulled his army back across the river to the fort at Detroit. The first invasion of Canada was over, less than four weeks after it began.

News Travels Slowly

News in 1812 traveled by horseback and boat. Word of Madison's June 18 declaration of war in Washington, D.C., reached New York City on June 21 and Boston, Massachusetts, on June 22. General William Hull received the message near Detroit on July 2. New Orleans heard on July 10. Americans guarding Fort Michilimackinac, between Lake Huron and Lake Michigan, learned that the United States was at war almost a month after it was declared, when British troops surrounded the fort on July 17.

THE NORTHWEST IN JEOPARDY

Meanwhile, at Fort Malden, Tecumseh and Major General Isaac Brock, the British commander in charge of Upper Canada, planned ways to scare Hull into surrendering Detroit. They wrote a letter to British troops at Fort Michilimackinac, requesting "only" 5,000 Native American reinforcements and made sure Hull's soldiers found it. On August 15, Brock sent a message directly to Hull, demanding the surrender of Detroit. He warned that he would not be able to control Tecumseh's warriors once a battle began. Brock wanted Hull to think that his Native American allies would not follow U.S. and British rules of war, which included imprisoning captives instead of killing them.

Hull refused to surrender, but his confidence was slipping. Since his return to Detroit, another detachment—this time 600 men—sent to escort the supply train from Ohio had been stopped by another ambush.

WEAPONS OF THE WAR OF 1812

Muskets The main weapon of the British and the U.S. infantries (foot soldiers), the musket *(below)* was an unreliable firearm that shot .7-inch lead balls 50 to 100 yards. To load a musket, the soldier first tore open a paper cartridge containing a ball and gunpowder. He sprinkled some of the powder on the flintlock pan at the back of the gun and the rest down its muzzle. Then he shoved the ball and the paper wrapping into the muzzle with a ramrod. The trigger released a hammer, which struck a flint, causing a spark that ignited the powder. The powder exploded and fired the ball. A skillful gunner could shoot three rounds a minute.

Bayonets Attached to the end of the musket, the bayonet *(below)* was a 21-inch pointed blade with two sharp edges. U.S. and British infantry units moved across a battlefield in lines two or three men deep, firing as they advanced, then rushed to the assault with the bayonet.

Rifles U.S. militiamen from the West carried "Kentucky rifles." Like muskets, rifles were muzzle-loaded and fired by a hammer striking flint. Although they shot smaller .4-inch balls, the rifle's longer bore (gun barrel) with spiral grooves sent the balls farther—300 yards or more—with greater accuracy. Rifles did not carry bayonets.

Swords U.S. and British officers carried swords as a symbol of rank and rarely used them in battle. An officer gave up his sword when surrendering.

Flintlock pistols Officers on both sides used pistols, if needed, in battle. Flintlock pistols *(right)* were fired in the same way as muskets and rifles. Sometimes the spark of the flint came in handy to fire the cannons when matches were lacking.

Cannons Cannons ranged in size from 4-pounders (which shot iron balls weighing 4 pounds) to 24- and 32-pounders. Small 4-pounders were used on battlefields and gunboats, while larger cannons were used on frigates and fortifications (defensive shelters). Cannons shot solid balls as far as 2,000 yards but were not very accurate. To fire a cannon, a gunner fed gunpowder down the cannon tube with a ladle on a long pole. The cannonball or other shot was loaded next. More gunpowder was sprinkled on a plate next to a touchhole, a hole in the base of the cannon. When a match was put to the gunpowder on the plate, the sparks flew into the touchhole and fired the gunpowder inside the cannon. The gunpowder exploded, sending the projectile out the mouth of the cannon. Before the cannon could be reloaded, the inside of the cannon tube had to be wiped out with a wet sponge to remove any residue. It generally took a crew of nine gunners to fire a cannon. If they took time to aim the gun, they could fire one or two rounds in a minute.

Carronades Shorter and lighter than cannons, carronades were used by both sides. Carronades fired projectiles with great force over a shorter range.

Congreve rockets First developed in 1805 by Sir William Congreve, these British rockets carried a charge of metal balls weighing 20 or more pounds. Large naval Congreve rockets might carry a charge as large as 320 pounds. Set off like firecrackers by lighting a fuse, rockets made a screaming noise and glowed red at night. They were useful for scaring soldiers and horses or for starting fires, but they could not be aimed with any accuracy. "Don't mind those rockets," U.S. general Jackson assured his artillerymen in New Orleans. "They are mere toys to amuse children." Only one person is known to have been killed by a Congreve rocket during the War of 1812.

Howitzers Smaller than cannons of the same caliber (the diameter of the barrel of a firearm), howitzers mounted on carriages were useful to both sides on battlefields.

Mortars Mortars lobbed balls or shells over high obstacles. The largest, used on British bomb ships, could launch 200-pound balls.

Hot shot Solid cannonballs heated in a furnace before firing were called hot shot. Their main use was to set fire to wooden buildings or ships.

Grapeshot Small iron balls tied to a wooden rod, grapeshot fired from a cannon had a shorter range (about 300 yards) than solid balls but scattered over a wider area.

Canister Musket balls placed in a tin cylinder were called canister shot. When shot from a cannon, the canister burst open and sent the musket balls flying to injure advancing troops at 200 yards.

Shrapnel Invented by Lieutenant Henry Shrapnel of the Royal Artillery in 1784, shrapnel was a round case full of small iron balls and an explosive charge. First used in the War of 1812 by the British at the Battle of Queenston, Ontario, shrapnel, like canister, could wound many soldiers when the case exploded.

Shells Shells were hollow metal balls filled with gunpowder. Shells had a wooden fuse, which was ignited when the powder in the gun exploded. The shell exploded only after the wooden fuse burned down. By then the shell would have reached its target.

U.S. general William Hull (*left*) surrendered Fort Detroit to British general Isaac Brock (*right, receiving sword*).

After Hull's refusal, the British began bombarding the U.S. fort from Sandwich, across the Detroit River, and from two warships on the river. That night, Tecumseh's 600 men quietly crossed the river to wait in the woods. At dawn, Brock and his 1,000 men also crossed and marched toward Detroit. To make his army appear more threatening, Brock had his militia wear the red jackets of the regular British soldiers. Tecumseh's war-painted troops meanwhile ran and whooped across an open space in the woods, then circled through the trees to do it again. Hull's officers reported 1,500 Native Americans. Then a cannon-ball pierced the wall of the fort and crashed through the officer's mess (dining room), killing four men.

Hull believed his troops were outnumbered. And he feared that if he lost, the Native Americans would massacre everyone, including innocent civilians sheltered in the fort—among them his own daughter and her children. Without firing a shot, he surrendered the fort and his entire army to the British.

The day before Hull's surrender, August 15, 70 Americans had evacuated Fort Dearborn in Illinois Territory, only to be attacked by 500 Potawatomi. About half of the men, women, and children there were killed. The rest were taken into captivity.

Americans leaving Fort Dearborn were attacked by Potawatomi warriors. Many Americans were killed, and the rest taken captive.

Two months into the war, instead of conquering Canada, the United States had lost three key forts that defended the northwestern territories: Fort Detroit on the eastern edge of Michigan, Fort Michilimackinac in the north, and Fort Dearborn in eastern Illinois Territory. The future states of Minnesota, Wisconsin, Illinois, and Michigan were in jeopardy.

USS CONSTITUTION

While the U.S. Army lost ground to the British, the U.S. Navy began to show its mettle. In July Captain Isaac Hull, the nephew of General William Hull, was sailing the *Constitution* up the Atlantic coast when he spied five British ships heading his way. In a dramatic chase lasting three days, Hull cleverly outmaneuvered his pursuers. Bostonians welcomed Hull as a hero when he sailed into Boston Harbor after his escape.

On August 19, during Hull's next voyage out, he met the *Guerrière,* one of the ships that had pursued the *Constitution* the month before. This time the *Guerrière* was alone. As the *Constitution* approached the *Guerrière,* both ships began delivering broadsides. For the *Constitution,* this meant 27 cannons going off in rapid succession; for the *Guerrière,* 25. Gunners on both ships reloaded and fired repeatedly at the enemy.

At first, neither ship caused much damage to the other. But when the *Constitution* drew closer, a shot from the U.S. frigate toppled one of the *Guerrière's* three masts. Then the *Constitution* drew ahead. Cutting across in front of the *Guerrière,* the *Constitution* swept the length of the *Guerrière's* decks with cannon fire. Quickly turning, it blasted the British ship with the guns on its other side. For a moment, the two ships tangled, the *Guerrière's* bow against the *Constitution's* stern (back end). Marines firing muskets from platforms on the masts of both ships picked off enemy gunners and prevented enemy marines from boarding their ship. Captain Hull's cabin caught fire, but Hull's crew quickly put it out.

When the ships came apart, the *Guerrière's* remaining two masts crashed down to the deck. Their weight rolled the *Guerrière* over, tipping it so far that half its

At sea the **USS** *Constitution* battled the British **HMS** *Guerrière* off the coast of Nova Scotia. In this print, the *Guerrière* has lost its masts.

guns dipped under the waves. The *Guerrière* was left "a perfect, unmanageable Wreck," her captain wrote in his official report. The *Constitution* was so little damaged, Captain Hull reported, that it could "be brought into action in two hours." After the British wounded and survivors were taken aboard the *Constitution,* what was left of the *Guerrière* was burned.

The victory greatly boosted American morale. A U.S. ship had bested the foremost naval power in the world. News of Isaac Hull's success helped offset disappointment over his uncle's surrender of Detroit, news that reached the East Coast the same day.

INVASION ACROSS THE NIAGARA

Meanwhile, in New York State, Senior Major General Henry Dearborn, a Revolutionary War veteran who had been given top military command over the U.S. Army, carried on with plans to invade Canada. The American Army of the Center was gathering along the Niagara River, a 36-mile-long waterway between Lake Erie and Lake Ontario. On the east bank of the river lay New York State, with Fort Niagara at the north end of the river and the villages of Buffalo and Black Rock at the south end.

On the west bank, in Upper Canada, the British Fort George faced Fort Niagara. The British Fort Erie threatened Buffalo and the U.S. naval base at Black Rock.

The invasion across the Niagara, however, was delayed by many problems. In September 1,000 New York militiamen waited in Lewiston, New York, for supplies and reinforcements. "Many lack shoes," their leader, Major General Stephen Van Rensselaer, complained. "All are clamorous [demanding] for pay; many are sick." When supplies and 1,700 more troops under Brigadier General Alexander Smyth finally arrived at the end of the month, however, Smyth and Van Rensselaer could not agree on where to attack.

In early October, while the senior officers debated strategy, naval lieutenant Jesse Elliott led 100 soldiers and sailors on a bold nighttime raid. Setting out from Black Rock, they rowed across the Niagara River and captured a British ship anchored under the protective guns of British Fort Erie. "GALLANT AND DARING EXPLOIT" crowed the headlines of the *Buffalo Gazette.*

Van Rensselaer decided it was time to act, even without Smyth's cooperation. Only a few regular troops under Lieutenant Colonel Winfield Scott joined Van Rensselaer as he initiated an attack on the village of Queenston on October 13. Smyth and the rest of his men remained in Buffalo.

Although the Americans began their invasion at 3 A.M., the British troops stationed in Queenston were not caught off guard. They fired on the small boats ferrying the U.S. troops across the Niagara River. Gunfire lit up the night sky, and a

U.S. troops crossed the Niagara River (above) to attack the Canadian village of Queenston. British reinforcements drove them back across the river.

booming cannon on a cliff above the village woke up General Isaac Brock, who was at Fort George, seven miles downriver.

The troops landed on a shore lined with redcoats (British troops) "as thick as bees upon a sugar maple." A few men found an unguarded path and scrambled up the cliff to capture the British cannon. Brock, who had galloped over from Fort George, led a charge up the slope to regain the gun. But his commanding presence made an easy target for the Americans, and he was quickly killed by a musket shot.

By midday, 600 Americans, led by Scott, held Queenston and the heights. When Van Rensselaer spotted more redcoats marching toward the village, he hurried back across the river to speed the ferrying of troops. But the remaining militia refused to get in the boats. They had seen enough of real war from the New York side of the

river. In despair, Van Rensselaer sent a message to Scott to retreat.

About 300 Mohawk, their faces masked with paint, began the counterattack, while 1,000 British troops formed a horseshoe-shaped line. When the redcoats advanced on Scott's men and drove them down to the riverbank, no boats waited to rescue them. Scott was forced to surrender.

After the battle, Van Rensselaer submitted his resignation, and Dearborn assigned Smyth the command of forces on the Niagara frontier. The second invasion of Canada had been even shorter than the first. The land war was turning into a disaster.

THE NAVY WINS A PRIZE

In October four U.S. ships sailed out of Boston Harbor "to do [their] utmost to annoy the enemy," as their sailing orders stated. Captain Stephen Decatur of the *United States* was nearing the Azores, islands in the North Atlantic Ocean about 800 miles west of Portugal, when he sighted the *Macedonian,* a 38-gun frigate, chasing him.

The *Macedonian* kept its distance at first, striking only with long guns and inflicting little damage. But the long guns on the *United States* were more powerful, and the Americans fired more quickly and with better aim. The *United States*'s cannonballs tore into the *Macedonian*'s sails and battered its hull.

Instead of fleeing, the *Macedonian* moved closer to use its shorter-range guns, or carronades. The *United*

EYEWITNESS QUOTE: CASUALTIES AT SEA

"I was busily supplying my gun with powder, when I saw blood suddenly fly from the arm of a man stationed at our gun . . . . The cries of the wounded now rang through all parts of the ship. These were carried to the cockpit as fast as they fell, while those more fortunate men, who were killed outright, were immediately thrown overboard."

—Samuel Leech, teenager on the *Macedonian,* October 1812

States pounded even harder, firing so rapidly that to the British it looked as though the *United States* was aflame. A U.S. carronade shot toppled one of the *Macedonian*'s masts and sliced the tops off the other two. Badly crippled and with most of its guns knocked off their carriages, the *Macedonian* finally surrendered. Her hull was pockmarked with 100 holes.

Crowds cheered Decatur when he sailed into New London, Connecticut, on December 4 with the *Macedonian,* the only British frigate ever brought as a prize of war into a U.S. port. The *Macedonian* was later displayed in New York Harbor, where Americans eager to

The U.S. warship *United States (right),* with its more powerful guns, defeated the British ship *Macedonian (left).*

Making Fun of Dearborn

Besides calling him "Granny," General Dearborn's troops made up songs about his military incompetence. One song, called "General, Glorious, Great, Granny Born-dear," goes:

> The war is commenc'd,
> And the army condens'd
> Devoid both of eating and fear
> They look for the presence;
> Of all soldiers, *the essence,*
> Of glorious, great, granny Born-dear.
>
> Some soldiers are freezing,
> Some coughing, some sneezing,
> Some laugh and cry out with a sneer,
> He never will come, for
> No one hates a drum more,
> Than glorious, great, granny Born-dear.

General "Granny" Dearborn

gloat over the United States' victory toured the captured ship.

THE INVASION POSTPONED

In November, although the long northern winter was approaching, U.S. military leaders still imagined that Canada could be conquered before year's end. In Plattsburgh, New York, the 61-year-old General Dearborn, whose troops called him "Granny," took command of 5,000 men and advanced into Lower Canada on November 19. But after only brief skirmishes with the British and one unfortunate incident of American detachments firing on one another, Dearborn decided to withdraw and put off conquering Canada until the spring.

In Buffalo, meanwhile, General Smyth issued proclamations promising a glorious invasion. On November 27, with a light snow falling and ice in the river, he loaded troops onto ships to cross the Niagara. But unwilling to act without the certainty of victory, he decided that he did not have enough men. When he loaded and unloaded his men again on December 1, the troops went wild with anger, even shooting musket balls into their general's tent. Smyth sent his militia home and his regular troops to winter quarters.

In contrast to the failures of the U.S. Army during the first six months of the war, the U.S. Navy had many successes. Although the Royal Navy captured three small U.S. ships, the U.S. Navy defeated three British frigates and four smaller naval ships. Better gunnery skills gave Americans the edge. Taking note of this uneven score, British ships were ordered not to cruise alone and to avoid challenging larger American ships.

THE PATTERN CHANGES

3

The year 1813 began with important shifts in Washington. Although still a less powerful political party, the Federalists won more local, state, and national elections in the fall of 1812. President Madison, however, had been reelected, and his Republican Party still had the most members in Congress. In response to criticism of how the war was going, Madison replaced both the secretary of war and the secretary of the navy in January 1813. Congress, which met from November 1812 to March 1813, voted to increase the size of the army and navy and to raise soldiers' wages.

"REMEMBER THE RAISIN!"

After the fall of Detroit in August 1812, Brigadier General William Henry Harrison had been given command of the new Army of the Northwest and was directed to recapture Detroit. But first, he had to secure the western frontier from Native American raiders. Endless rain in October and November had made it impossible to move heavy guns and supplies over muddy roads from southern Ohio toward Detroit. In northwestern Ohio, meanwhile, General James Winchester and his Kentucky militia waited for supplies and orders at Fort Winchester. In summer cottons worn to rags, with only scraps of blankets to keep them warm, the men got by on half rations (food portions) and nuts.

When winter finally froze the muddy roads, Harrison was in Upper Sandusky, Ohio, ready to gather his troops and move north to attack Fort Malden. On January 10, Winchester marched 1,300 half-starved

Kentuckians through the snow to the rendezvous point at the Maumee rapids.

Before Harrison arrived, however, two men from the area requested protection for Americans in French-town, a village 30 miles away on the Raisin River. The town (part of modern-day Monroe, Michigan) had been occupied by a small force of Canadian militia and Native Americans, and about 600 Kentuckians went to rescue it. They defeated the enemy, but a dozen were killed and more than 50 men were wounded. Winchester brought rein-forcements to secure the town from further attacks.

The British at Fort Malden took the opportunity to surprise the Americans at Frenchtown. Led by Lieutenant Colonel Henry Proctor, British and Native American troops hauled heavy artillery 20 miles across the Lake Erie ice. Before dawn on January 21, Proctor and his men began positioning cannon to fire on the U.S. camp.

Alerted by their sentries (lookouts), the U.S. troops opened fire first, but the men camped outside the village lacked cover. Driven back, they found the snow too deep for running. Many were caught, killed, and scalped.

When Winchester was captured by a Wyandot chief, he ordered a surrender to prevent more bloodshed. After the battle,

---

EYEWITNESS QUOTE: THE KENTUCKY MILITIA

"**Their appearance was miserable. . . . It was the depth of winter; but scarcely an individual was in possession of a great coat or cloak, and few of them wore garments of wool of any description. . . . They were covered with slouch hats, worn bare by constant use, beneath which their long hair fell matted and uncombed over their cheeks . . . dirty blankets [were] wrapped around their loins.**"

—Major John Richardson, British officer at Frenchtown, 1813

Proctor returned to Fort Malden because he feared Harrison was on his way with a large army. Proctor left the wounded prisoners behind with a few British guards.

That night, many Native Americans, enflamed by alcohol and the desire for revenge, returned to plun-der the village. The helpless U.S. prisoners "were toma-hawked, and many were burned alive in the houses," U.S. officers reported later. The bloody battle and the massacre roused U.S. anger. "Remember the Raisin" became the rallying cry for U.S. troops, especially those from Kentucky, for the remainder of the war.

The disaster brought Harrison's winter campaign to a close. As the U.S. Army awaited orders, Harrison devoted his considerable energy to build-ing Fort Meigs at the foot of the rapids on the Maumee River in Ohio.

THE BRITISH NAVY TAKES CONTROL

As the year 1813 began, two ships contin-ued the winning streak for the U.S. Navy. On February 14, Captain James Lawrence on the sloop of war (small warship) *Hornet* captured a British brig (two-masted, square-rigged ship), the *Resolution,* with $23,000 in cash aboard. Ten days later, off the coast of South America, Lawrence sank another British brig, the *Peacock,* after a brief battle.

SOLDIERS AND UNIFORMS

U.S. Soldiers U.S. soldiers were either regulars, who served full-time for several years, or militiamen, able-bodied men who trained for a few days each year and could be called up in emergencies by the state governor for a short period of time. When the war began, few soldiers had either experience or training. The army's best hope were the westerners, who owned rifles, were used to hardships, and had fought against Native Americans. Kentucky riflemen were said to be able to shoot the whiskers off a squirrel 300 yards away. They were eager for battle, but not yet accustomed to the discipline of army life. Farm boys from east of the Appalachians were less familiar with firearms. They were also less eager for battle and worried that their tour of duty, which might be as little as three months, might interfere with planting or harvesting their crops. Many militiamen from eastern states, claiming that the Constitution required them to serve only in their home states, refused to cross the border into Canada.

Regular soldiers who had uniforms wore white trousers and blue single-breasted jackets with a high collar *(shown at left)*. A black bucket-shaped hat topped off the uniform. The British blockade soon created shortages of cloth, however, and uniforms were made of whatever color cloth was available. Militiamen wore whatever they had. The westerners were especially picturesque in their coonskin hats and fringed deerskin. Easterners might be dressed in homespun fabric. By 1814 uniforms were so scarce that some militia recruits had only a red scarf tied around their heads to identify them as soldiers.

British Soldiers British soldiers were part of a long tradition of military service. Many regulars had served in Europe, Asia, or the West Indies before coming to Canada. Tough and disciplined, they were well trained in European battlefield tactics, although less used to fighting in woods. Their double-breasted red coats *(right)* had a variety of trimmings that identified their regiment and branch of service. Otherwise, their white trousers and black hats resembled those worn by U.S. regulars.

For the British soldier, war was usually a chosen career, not a temporary interruption of his life.

Canadian Militia Like the U.S. militia, the Canadian militia was generally made up of farmers, not soldiers. They benefited, however, from strong British leadership and example. Many were skilled in marksmanship and forest fighting. The Canadians were defending their homes and farms from U.S. invaders, so they took the war seriously. They could be as forceful in battle as the British regulars.

The Navy The differences between U.S. and British servicemen were less obvious in the navies of the two countries. U.S. sailors were more experienced and better trained than U.S. soldiers. Some sailors had fought against pirates in North Africa. Others had been impressed and had served aboard British naval ships. Even U.S. and British uniforms were alike *(below):* blue jackets, white trousers, and round black hats. During battles, however, both sides stripped down, going barefoot and shirtless in order to move quickly. On both sides, being a seaman was a lifetime career, although some men had also served on merchant ships as well as in the navy.

Marines British and U.S. marines wore military uniforms, since they were basically soldiers who served aboard ships. During naval battles, they fired their muskets on the enemy from platforms high up on the masts. If an enemy ship came close enough, marines boarded the enemy ship to continue the battle with swords and firearms. British marines dressed in red coats with blue trim. U.S. marines wore green coats with white trim. Like the sailors, U.S. marines had gained war experience fighting pirates on the shores of Tripoli in Africa and took a professional pride in military service.

Privateers

U.S. naval vessels were not alone in the "economic war" on the high seas. The United States also hired private ships, called privateers, to attack enemy merchant ships. When a privateer was captured, crews offered documents called "letters of marque and reprisal," which saved them from being executed as pirates. Instead, crew members became prisoners of war and could be exchanged for British prisoners of war. If a privateer won a battle, the enemy ship and its cargo was its prize.

The smaller U.S. privateer ship the *Decatur* captures a British merchant ship.

Privateering ships were typically armed with one Long Tom (a 12- or 24-pound cannon) and a few smaller guns. A ship's main weapon was speed. Called clippers, these slender, light-hulled vessels with tilted masts specialized in quick strikes and speedy retreats. They preyed on British shipping between the West Indies and Canada and also across the Atlantic off the coasts of England and Ireland.

The 515 American privateers operating during the War of 1812 captured about 1,345 prizes. Although 148 privateering ships were lost, most had already more than paid for the loss by the capture of many valuable prizes.

The *Essex,* a small U.S. frigate weighed down with 44 guns, also met success. In January Captain David Porter sailed the *Essex* around Cape Horn (the tip of South America) to the Pacific. It was a risky business. Americans could not count on finding friendly ports for supplies or repairs because both Portugal and Spain, countries that had colonized many of the countries and islands of the Pacific, were allied with Britain.

The intrepid Porter nevertheless managed to spend the next 18 months attacking British whaling ships. He never needed to worry about supplies because his prizes provided food, sails, ropes, anchors, spare parts, guns, ammunition, medicines, and even the money he needed to pay his men. Without meeting a British warship in battle, the *Essex* helped the war effort by hurting the British economy.

Many other U.S. ships—including the *Constitution,* the *United States,* and the prize ship *Macedonian*—spent the spring and summer trapped in U.S. harbors as the British navy sent more ships from Europe to enforce its blockade of U.S. ports. By February, 17 British ships of the line (large warships), which were larger than any U.S. ship, two 50-gun ships, 27 frigates, and about 50 smaller vessels were patrolling U.S. waters.

The British warships used their naval advantage to attack small, poorly defended towns along the shores of Virginia, Maryland, Delaware, the Carolinas, and Georgia. Led by Rear Admiral Sir George Cockburn, the British took possession of small coastal islands with farms to provide food for the British fleet. They raided along the coast, into bays, and up rivers, looting and burning towns, destroying a cannon manufacturer, seizing gunboats and small ships, and terrorizing people living on the waterfronts.

THE CAPTURE OF YORK

When spring arrived and the ice broke up on the Great Lakes, the campaign to conquer Canada resumed. During the fall and winter, Commodore Isaac Chauncey had assembled a small fleet at Sackets Harbor, New York. In April it carried 1,700 American troops across Lake Ontario to York, the provincial capital of Upper Canada (modern-day Toronto). The commander of the expedition was Brigadier General Zebulon Pike.

With gale-force winds blowing, the U.S. force landed slightly west of York on April 27. A small number of British and Native Americans fired on U.S. invaders, but soon retreated when guns on the U.S. boats returned fire. The British regrouped at a battery west of the town. There, their powder magazine (a warehouse of gunpowder) accidentally blew up and forced them to retreat into Fort York. Realizing that his men could not hold the town, the British general, Sir Roger Sheaffe, set fuses to blow up the fort and fled with his troops. To keep the Americans from realizing the fort was abandoned, the British did not lower the flag in surrender.

> **BATTERIES**
> A battery is a grouping of artillery pieces—cannons, mortars, and howitzers—placed at a strategic point to attack an enemy.

FAST FACT

The Americans were just outside the fort when the magazine exploded. Earth, stone, and timber flew in every direction. A boulder crashed down on General Pike,

Military Glory

Zebulon Pike was not afraid to die for his country. In a letter to his father before the Battle of York, the 34-year-old soldier wrote: "If success attends my steps, honor and glory await my name—if defeat, still it shall be said we died like brave men; and conferred honor, even in death, on the American Name."

An illustration of the death of General Zebulon Pike at the Battle of York in Canada

who died of his wounds. Hundreds of soldiers were killed or injured.

Reacting in anger, the Americans set fire to the public buildings in York and looted private houses left empty by families fleeing the battle. The Americans left York six days later, returning across Lake Ontario with a 10-gun British brig to add to Chauncey's fleet and a large quantity of British military supplies.

DEFENDING FORT MEIGS

In late April, Proctor (by then a British major general) and Tecumseh invaded northern Ohio and laid siege to Fort Meigs on the Maumee River. As British guns lobbed cannonballs over the walls, General Harrison and a small garrison waited for reinforcements.

On May 5, two regiments of Kentucky militia crossed the turbulent rapids behind the fort, landed on the opposite bank, and charged the British battery. The gunners ran off, and the Americans quickly disabled the guns by jamming metal rods into the touchholes, where the guns were ignited. Instead of returning to the boats, the Americans chased after Tecumseh's men, who were shooting at them from the forest. The warriors lured them deeper into the woods before turning, firing their muskets, and attacking the fallen Americans with tomahawks and scalping knives. Many surviving Kentuckians were captured by the British, and only a few made it safely to the fort. At the end of the day, however, the Americans still held Fort Meigs.

After the battle, 600 U.S. prisoners were marched to the British camp. There Native Americans yanked off their hats, clothing, money, and watches and forced them through a double line of warriors, who prodded or struck them with clubs. When a British officer tried to protect the Americans, a Native American shot him dead. As the prisoners watched in horror, Potawatomi warriors began calmly shooting and scalping one American after another.

During this slaughter, Tecumseh rode into the camp and dismissed the Native Americans with angry words. His rescue of the prisoners became a legend. In one version of the story, he scolded Proctor for not preventing the massacre, saying, "I conquer to save, and you to murder!" In another version, Proctor replied that the Native Americans could not be controlled.

Tecumseh *(left)* drove off the Potawatomi warriors after they had killed many of the surrendered U.S. soldiers. He blamed British general Henry Proctor *(right)* for not stopping the massacre.

"Begone!" Tecumseh shouted, "You are unfit to command. Go and put on petticoats!"

A few days later, the British gave up the siege. Most of the Native Americans had left with their stolen goods, and the Canadian militia demanded to return home to plant their crops.

CROSSING THE NIAGARA

At the end of May, General Dearborn was ready to capture British Fort George near Newark, Ontario. For three days, U.S. guns at Fort Niagara bombarded Newark. Then at 4 A.M. on May 27, 4,500 U.S. troops boarded Commodore Chauncey's fleet to cross the river.

Dearborn himself was ill and watched the battle through a telescope from the deck of the *Madison*. Winfield Scott, by then a full colonel, directed the landing, assisted by Oliver Hazard Perry, the naval commodore who two months earlier had taken command of the U.S. fleet on Lake Erie.

In a stiff wind, the men rowed ashore in small boats, protected by the guns on Chauncey's ships. The British formed a line of battle west of the fort. Finding themselves outnumbered and outgunned, they retreated toward Queenston. The British commandant, Brigadier General John Vincent, ordered all the other Niagara garrisons—Queenston, Chippewa, and Fort Erie—to evacuate as well. The Americans at last held both sides of the Niagara River.

ATTACK ON SACKETS HARBOR

While Chauncey's fleet was busy at Fort George, the British took advantage of its absence from Sackets Harbor. Sir George Prevost, governor general and commander in chief of the British forces in Canada, sailed across Lake Ontario from the British naval base at Kingston with 750 troops. Warned by a scout of a possible attack, Brigadier General Jacob Brown fired signal guns to call his militia from nearby towns to help the few regular soldiers at the U.S. naval base.

The British landed on the morning of May 29. Militiamen waiting on the beach fired on them, but they fled as the bayonet-wielding redcoats advanced. The regular U.S. troops put up a stiffer opposition. Their steady fire dismayed the British. Shot "flew like hail," a British soldier said later.

Seeing his men unable to advance farther, the British commander ordered a retreat. "Had not General Prevost retired *most rapidly* under the guns of his vessels," Brown wrote in his official report, "he would never have returned to Kingston." For his leadership that day, Jacob Brown was promoted from brigadier general of the militia to brigadier general of the regular army.

Fleeing Militia

At the Battle of Sackets Harbor, General Jacob Brown tricked fleeing militia into returning to the battle by sending mounted soldiers after them with news of a victory. When the men came back, Brown chewed them out and sent them back to the front.

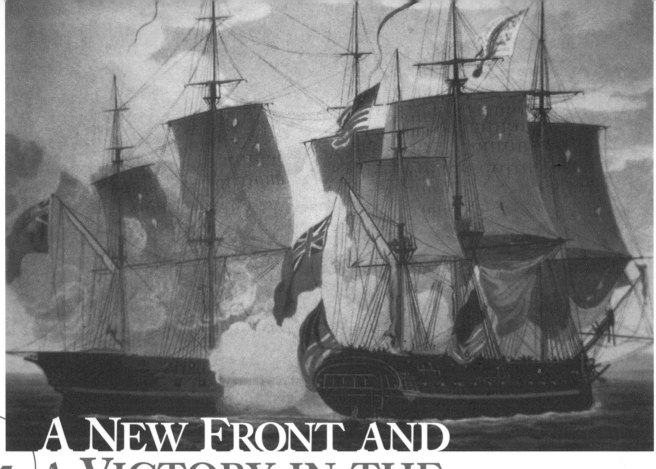

A NEW FRONT AND
4 A VICTORY IN THE NORTHWEST

As the first anniversary of the war's start approached, Americans were encouraged by the successes of the spring campaign. The news from York, Fort Meigs, Fort George, and Sackets Harbor suggested that the U.S. Army was gaining experience and skill. But there were problems for the U.S. Navy at sea, and a new front opened in the South.

"DON'T GIVE UP THE SHIP"

On June 1, 1813, a fine summer day, the *Chesapeake* proudly sailed out of Boston Harbor flying a banner that read "Free Trade and Sailor's Rights." Guarding the entrance to the harbor stood the *Shannon,* a British frigate with 52 guns.

Neither ship tried to avoid a battle, but they drew together for a duel, both firing rapidly. Captain James Lawrence on the *Chesapeake* was soon badly wounded, but he urged his crew to carry on. "Don't give up the ship!" he told his men as they carried him below decks. The *Chesapeake,* however, lost a sail, which caused it to veer away from the *Shannon.* The movement exposed its stern to destructive gunfire by the British ship. Many U.S. officers and seamen were struck down.

Captain Philip Broke of the HMS *Shannon* leads British marines onto the *Chesapeake* and captures the U.S. ship.

The two ships then tangled, and Captain Philip Broke of the *Shannon,* his sword drawn, led his marines onto the *Chesapeake* for a hand-to-hand struggle. With their losses mounting, the Americans surrendered. The entire bloody battle had lasted 15 minutes. Captain Lawrence died, and Captain Broke was badly wounded.

After the many naval victories, the loss of the *Chesapeake* was a sobering defeat. While the British celebrated, Lawrence received a hero's funeral in New York City, "reportedly attended by 50,000 people." His last words to his crew, "Don't give up the ship!" became the motto of the U.S. Navy.

THE CREEK REBEL

During the summer, unrest broke out among Native American groups in the South. Before the war, the Creek Nation had lived peacefully with white settlers. When Tecumseh traveled to Mississippi Territory in 1811 to spread his idea of a united Indian nation, however, he found many Creek who resented U.S. expansion.

In the fall of 1812, several young Creek warriors went north to visit Prophetstown and took part in the battle at Frenchtown in January 1813. On their way home in February, they murdered two white families who had settled near the mouth of the Ohio River.

Creek elders, appalled by what the group had done, hunted down and killed the young men. But many other rebellious Creek grew angry at the elders' action. Calling themselves the Red Sticks for their red-painted war clubs, they vowed to avenge the slain warriors. The Creek Nation soon split into two violent groups.

In July 1813, the Red Sticks gathered in present-day central Alabama and planned war on U.S. settlers. A group of warriors went to Pensacola, Florida, to ask the Spanish for weapons and ammunition. As the Red Sticks returned with a pack train of mules carrying supplies, a band of

The Red Sticks of the Creek Nation attacked Fort Mims and killed most of the people who had taken refuge there.

Mississippi militiamen attacked. The Creek chased off their attackers, but the Americans captured many of the pack mules.

To avenge their losses, the Red Sticks stormed Fort Mims in southern Alabama on August 30. Although the fort was crowded with families who had gone there for refuge, the gates had been left open. Everyone was having dinner when the Red Sticks, their faces painted red and black, rushed in. In the fighting that followed, the Americans retreated to various buildings within the stockade, which the Red Sticks set on fire. Almost all of the people in the fort, including women and children, were killed, mutilated, and scalped. A few whites had escaped, and some African American slaves were spared to become slaves for the Red Sticks.

For the United States, the Creek rebellion was a serious threat to the security of the South. The Red Sticks would have to be defeated before they joined forces with the British as Tecumseh had done in the Northwest.

BATTLE OF LAKE ERIE

Shortly after the massacre at Fort Mims, the war in the North took a new turn. On Lake Erie, Commodore Perry had assembled a fleet at Erie, Pennsylvania. Five new ships had been built during the spring and summer. Four other ships had been brought up Lake Erie from Black Rock, New York. Perry was watching for a chance to challenge the British when six British ships, commanded by Captain Robert Barclay, sailed into view on September 10.

Aboard the 20-gun flagship (the ship that carries the commander of the fleet) *Lawrence,* named for the heroic captain of the *Chesapeake,* Perry hoisted a banner stitched with Lawrence's words, "DON'T GIVE UP THE SHIP." The whole fleet cheered.

When the *Lawrence* was disabled, Commodore Oliver Hazard Perry, carrying his ship's battle flag, was rowed to the *Niagara*. Commanding from this ship, he defeated the British navy on Lake Erie.

The British opened fire first, damaging the *Lawrence.* Moving closer, Perry was soon fighting off the two largest British ships, the *Detroit,* with 21 guns, and the *Queen Charlotte,* with 18. Perry's seven smaller vessels were firing on the smaller British ships. But the United States' 20-gun ship, *Niagara,* commanded by Jesse Elliott, held back, using only its long guns to assist in the battle.

British cannonballs shredded the *Lawrence*'s rigging and sails, shattered its decks, disabled its guns, and struck down its crew. Unwilling to surrender, Perry lowered a boat and, carrying the battle flag with him, was rowed to the *Niagara* through a hailstorm of enemy fire.

EYEWITNESS QUOTE:
BATTLE OF LAKE ERIE

"It was a time of conflicting emotions when [Perry] stepped upon the deck. The battle was won and he was safe, but the deck was slippery with blood, and strewn with the bodies of twenty officers and men. . . . Those of us who were spared and able to walk met [Perry] at the gangway to welcome him on board, but the salutation was a silent one."

—Dr. Usher Parsons, after the Battle of Lake Erie, September 1813

Taking charge of the *Niagara,* Perry cut through the British line, striking all six British ships by firing the carronades on both sides of the ship. Badly damaged, the *Detroit* and the *Queen Charlotte* tangled together, and Perry turned the *Niagara*'s guns on them both. After three hours of battle, Barclay surrendered. His two largest ships were destroyed, and his six captains killed or wounded.

On the back of an old letter, Perry wrote a message to General Harrison: "We have met the enemy and they are ours." Perry's stunning victory gave the United States control of Lake Erie and a chance to regain the humiliating losses of 1812.

MEDICAL CARE

Army and navy doctors during the War of 1812 had to treat many contagious diseases that broke out in crowded, unsanitary military camps and on ships. Dysentery, typhoid, pneumonia, malaria, measles, mumps, and smallpox killed far more men than bullets or cannonballs. In a camp near Plattsburgh in December 1812, so many men were ill that they "made the very woods ring with coughing and groaning."

An extract from the bark of the cinchona tree was helpful in curing malaria. But most of the available medicines and therapies did not help the sick. Doctors often used emetics (which cause vomiting) or cathartics (which cause diarrhea) to "cleanse the stomach." These medicines did clear out the digestive system, mainly because they were very toxic. One popular cathartic, calomel (mercurous chloride), caused mercury poisoning. Another, niter, or saltpeter, dangerously slowed the heart rate. Treatment left patients weak and dehydrated.

Doctors also drained blood from patients to reduce fevers. Most doctors believed that bloodletting helped only if the patient bled until he fainted. The therapy might be repeated over several days, often speeding the patient's death.

Treatment for those who were wounded in battle consisted mainly of amputating shattered limbs and trepanning (drilling holes in) skulls to relieve the pressure of head wounds.

An amputation saw

After hundreds of soldiers were wounded in the explosion at York in April 1813, Dr. William Beaumont wrote in his journal about how, "wading in blood," he "cut & slashed for 48 hours without food or sleep."

To get through the agony of surgery without anesthetics, patients were given only opium or alcohol.

A trephine was used to relieve pressure in the skull from head wounds.

Although deep wounds sometimes became seriously infected, patients generally recovered from amputations and surface wounds.

BATTLE OF THE THAMES

With Lake Erie secured, Harrison's army was ready to march on Fort Malden in order to retake Detroit. A regiment of mounted Kentucky sharpshooters (skilled, accurate shooters) led by congressman-turned-major Richard M. Johnson joined the campaign.

When Harrison arrived on September 27, however, Fort Malden was a smoldering heap of charred wood. General Proctor had retreated up the Thames River valley. Before leaving, Tecumseh had argued with Proctor. "We are determined to defend our lands," he said, "and if it is [the Great Spirit's] will, we wish to leave our bones upon them." He had accompanied the British on the understanding that there would be a battle.

After restoring Detroit to U.S. rule, Harrison set out after Proctor, with Johnson's mounted regiment in the advance, setting a rapid pace through the rain-soaked forests. As the Americans narrowed the gap, Proctor chose a battle site near Moraviantown, Ontario. On October 5, he placed his redcoats in a double line across the road on either side of a small swamp and into the woods on either side. To their left ran the Thames River. To their right lay a swamp, where, on a strip of dry ground, Tecumseh and his warriors hid among the decaying trees.

Warned of the British position, Harrison lined up his troops out of range of British fire and gave Johnson permission to lead the charge. Dividing his regiment in two, Johnson ordered half to attack the redcoats and half to attack Tecumseh's men.

The bugle sounded the charge. "Remember the Raisin!" resounded as the Kentuckians spurred their horses through the trees. The redcoats fired, but the Kentuckians rode right through both lines before the British had time to reload. Seeing the horsemen galloping toward his command center behind the lines, Proctor fled.

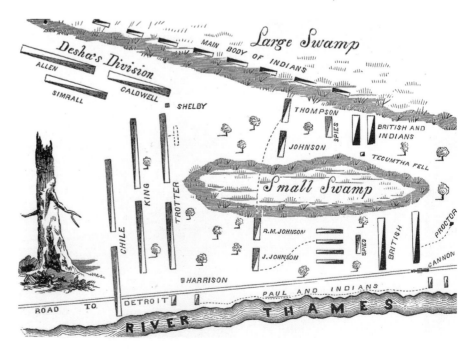

This map of troop positions in the Battle of the Thames shows British troops led by Proctor on the right, Native Americans lined up in the large swamp and by the Thames River, and U.S. troops advancing from the left.

The Kentuckians turned, took aim, and attacked the British line from the rear while Harrison's infantry closed in from the front. Trapped, the British surrendered.

Fighting against the Native Americans was tougher. The Kentuckians sent out 20 volunteers to attract enemy fire, then charged into battle. When their horses became stuck in the mud, the Kentuckians jumped down and fought hand-to-hand using tomahawks and knives. The infantry moved in with muskets.

The bloody battle raged for almost an hour. Then the Americans noticed that Tecumseh's war cries no longer echoed above the crackle of gunfire. The ranks of Native Americans thinned. The firing dropped off, and as the gun smoke cleared, the Americans saw that they held the field. Tecumseh had been killed, and his followers had carried his body away.

The brief engagement was an important turning point in the war. It did not push the British out of Upper Canada, but it saved the future states of Indiana, Illinois, Wisconsin, and Michigan, not only from the British but also from Native American retaliation. Tecumseh's dream of a united Native American nation ended with his death at the Battle of the Thames.

MISSION: MONTREAL

As fall began, the United States created a new invasion plan. Dearborn's replacement, Brigadier General James Wilkinson, was to travel down the St. Lawrence River from Sackets Harbor with 7,000 men. Major General Wade Hampton was to march north from the Lake Champlain

"Forlorn Hope"

The tactic that Johnson's mounted regiment used at the Battle of the Thames was called the "Forlorn Hope" by both the British and the Americans. A small group was sent out first to attract enemy fire. While the enemy reloaded their muskets—getting the gunpowder and ball into place took about 20 seconds—the rest of the troops attacked.

Johnson himself took part in the Forlorn Hope at the Battle of the Thames. Out of the squad of 20 Americans, 15 were killed or mortally wounded in the attack. Johnson survived to become a popular hero. He later claimed that he had shot Tecumseh. In 1837 he became the ninth vice president of the United States.

valley with 4,500 men. The two armies were to meet up and attack Montreal.

In October Hampton's troops began an advance along the Chateaugay River, which runs from northern New York State to the St. Lawrence River in Canada. They were stopped by Canadian militia and retreated to the New York side of the border.

In early November, Wilkinson's troops set out from French Creek, New York, at the Lake Ontario end of the St. Lawrence River in 350 boats. The journey was not easy. Batteries of British guns and sharpshooters guarded the river, and a small British fleet threatened the rear. The U.S. troops disembarked and camped on shore at night, while detachments were sent downstream to clear the Canadian riverbank. The two sides clashed on November 11, but the British were unable to stop the U.S. advance.

The great chief Tecumseh was killed at the Battle of the Thames, near Moraviantown, Ontario.

What the British failed to do, the Americans did themselves. On November 12, Wilkinson received a letter from Hampton full of excuses for not meeting him—muddy roads, exhausted troops, low supplies. Furious at Hampton, Wilkinson called off the campaign just three days from Montreal.

NIAGARA IN FLAMES

As the U.S. Army focused on Montreal, only a few hundred Americans, most of them militiamen, guarded the forts and towns along the Niagara River. Hearing that the British were approaching to recapture Fort George, General George McClure ordered an evacuation on December 10. Before the U.S. troops boarded the boats to carry them across to Fort Niagara, on the New York side of the river, McClure ordered the village of Newark burned, leaving villagers homeless in the snow.

The following week, the British slipped across the river in the early morning and surprised the small garrison at Fort Niagara. Without firing a shot, they took about 350 prisoners and killed 67 others with their bayonets.

In retaliation for McClure's burning of Newark, the British raided towns all along the river. On December 29, they vanquished the militia guarding the naval station at Black Rock and torched Buffalo and Black Rock along with army storehouses and naval schooners (two-masted ships) in the harbor. The fire spread so widely that only three houses were left standing.

THE CREEK VANQUISHED, THE LAST INVASION

5

After the massacre at Fort Mims in August 1813, the United States was engaged in two wars: against Britain and against hostile Creek. Settling the Creek War was crucial because the war with Britain was growing more serious. During 1813 Britain and its allies had been gaining ground against Napoleon in Europe. After Napoleon surrendered in April 1814, Britain was free to focus all its military power on its unruly former colony.

Meanwhile, in the U.S. Army, younger leaders were replacing the Revolutionary War veterans. The militia had become more dependable and better trained. Two years of war had hardened and seasoned the troops.

DEFEATING THE RED STICKS

In mid-March 1814, General Andrew Jackson set out from Fort Strother in northern Alabama with 3,000 men. Several hundred Cherokee and Creek guided Jackson's army to the Red Sticks' base of operations on a peninsula, called Horseshoe Bend, formed by a loop on the Tallapoosa River. High log breastworks zigzagged across the neck of the peninsula.

BREASTWORKS

Breastworks are walls built to defend a place. Men and cannons placed along the breastworks can fire down on approaching troops.

FAST FACT

To the rear, canoes provided a means of escape for the Red Sticks.

On March 27, Jackson placed part of his army across the river behind the fort and began firing his field guns at the breastworks. The cannonballs did not harm the stout log wall, however. Meanwhile, the friendly Native Americans swam across the river to steal the canoes and set fires inside the fort to distract the defenders. Seizing the moment, Jackson's men stormed the barricade, clambering over the logs under a hail of arrows and bullets.

Inside, the Red Sticks were trapped as troops closed in from the front and the rear. Jackson's men remained until nightfall, killing the Red Sticks and setting fire to all the buildings. Even Jackson admitted later to his wife that the "carnage was dreadfull."

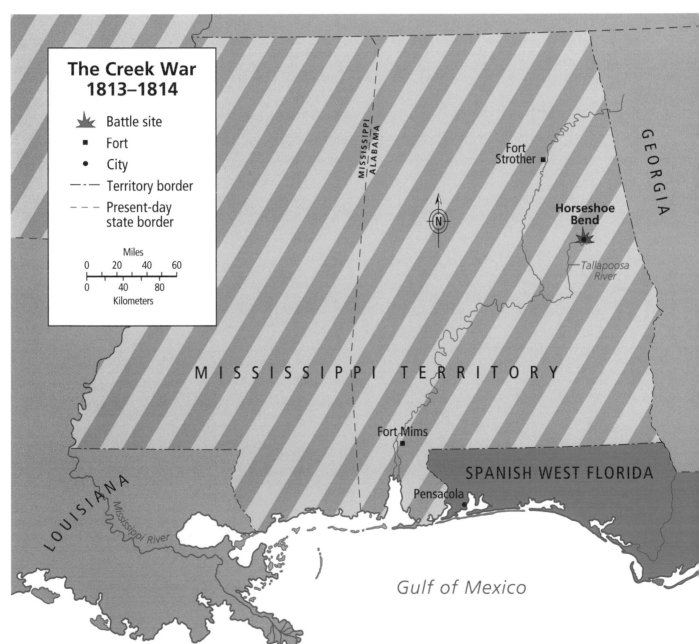

The Creek War 1813–1814

⭐ Battle site
■ Fort
● City
–·–·– Territory border
– – – Present-day state border

Miles
0   20   40   60
0   40   80
Kilometers

MISSISSIPPI / ALABAMA

Fort Strother ■

Horseshoe Bend ⭐

Tallapoosa River

GEORGIA

MISSISSIPPI TERRITORY

Fort Mims ■

SPANISH WEST FLORIDA

Pensacola ●

LOUISIANA

Mississippi River

Gulf of Mexico

General Andrew Jackson

had been drilling his brigade seven to ten hours a day.

On July 3, the Americans crossed the Niagara River from Buffalo and Black Rock and closed in on Fort Erie from two sides. The small British garrison at first fired on the approaching troops, but seeing themselves surrounded by an army of 3,500 men, they surrendered.

The next day, the Americans moved 12 miles north along the Niagara River to a British outpost at Chippewa. On July 5, late in the afternoon, British troops advanced toward the U.S. camp. One unit entered the woods parallel to the Niagara River. Another formed double lines across an open field alongside the river. A regiment of Pennsylvania militia and Iroquois sent to clear the woods of skirmishers spotted the redcoats and dashed back to the U.S. camp.

SKIRMISHERS

Special troops, called flanking companies or skirmishers, patrolled an area around a military camp or march. They did not carry heavy packs so that they could move quickly to wherever they were needed or to warn the main army of enemy movements.

FAST FACT

After the battle, Jackson was promoted to brigadier general of the U.S. Army and given command of the Gulf Coast region. The treaty ending the Creek War was signed on August 9, 1814. Surviving hostile Creek had fled to Florida. Jackson forced the friendly Creek who had helped the war effort to sign an agreement that gave the United States 23 million acres of Creek land—more than half their territory.

THE LAST INVASION OF CANADA

While Jackson secured U.S. forts in the South, Major General Jacob Brown had gathered an army in Buffalo to invade Canada across the Niagara River. His best troops were those trained by Winfield Scott, promoted to brigadier general, who

Scott was just marching his men out to drill when Brown galloped past with the warning, "You will have a battle!" Scott quickly spread out his troops in three battalions (large companies of troops) and advanced them toward the British line in the open field. With cool precision, his well-drilled men repeatedly halted, fired, and advanced. On his right, American field guns blazed at the British cannons. On his

A U.S. officer and troops capture enemy cannon at the British outpost of Chippewa on the Niagara River.

left, in the woods, the militia and Native Americans returned to the fighting together with the rest of the regulars.

As the opposing forces got closer, Scott angled his outer battalions toward the edges of the British line. With Americans firing at them from both the front and the sides, the redcoats wavered.

British officers quickly organized a retreat. Although many British escaped to a blockhouse (military building with holes cut into the walls to shoot through) on the far side of the Niagara River, the Americans won a decisive victory. Scott's achievement was especially celebrated because it was the first time in the war that approximately equal numbers of U.S. and British troops had fought on an open plain in daylight.

Regulars in Gray

By 1814 the U.S. Army in Buffalo had run out of blue cloth for making uniforms. Supply officers provided Winfield Scott's troops with gray jackets to go with their white trousers. The British general opposing Scott at Chippewa thought at first that he was fighting U.S. militia instead of regular troops. When he saw how disciplined the Americans were in their attack, however, he exclaimed, "Those are regulars, by God!"

Scott's men fought so well in the campaign that to honor them, gray jackets became the uniform worn by students at the U.S. Military Academy at West Point, New York.

MINORITIES IN THE WAR OF 1812

All of the officers and most of the enlisted men and militiamen were white Americans of European descent. Two groups of minorities, Native Americans and African Americans, played significant roles in the War of 1812.

Many Native Americans followed Tecumseh in joining the British side of the war, but others aided the U.S. cause, often by working as scouts or guides. Eleazer Williams, who was of mixed Caughnawaga and Anglo-American blood, organized a team of rangers, who supplied information to troops in New York State. Although he didn't believe in war, he considered it his patriotic duty to help recruit Native Americans, among them members of the St. Regis Nation, who were put to work making snowshoes for the army.

The Iroquois chief Red Jacket (left) raised Native American troops for the Americans. After the Battle of Chippewa, however, as the Iroquois fighting for the U.S. side scoured the woods for their dead and wounded comrades, they found many friends and relatives who had fought on the British side. Red Jacket decided that the white man's dispute was not worth the destruction of his own nation. He held a council in Burlington, Ontario, where Iroquois who had joined the British agreed with his proposal to withdraw from the war.

Mohawk, Oneida, Wyandot, Shawnee, Seneca, Choctaw, Chickasaw, and Creek also served alongside U.S. troops in battle. Many other Native Americans, however, both in the United States and Canada, remained neutral.

Large numbers of free, nonslave African Americans served in the U.S. Navy, forming about one-sixth of the total naval personnel. Crews were fully integrated, and no mention of racial origin appears in naval records. In his official report of the battle between the *Constitution* and the *Guerrière,* Captain Isaac Hull singled out his black sailors for special praise: "I never had any better fighters . . . they stripped to the waist and fought like devils, sir . . . utterly insensible to danger & . . . possessed with a determination to outfight white sailors."

An African American sailor accompanied Oliver Perry as he transferred his command from the *Lawrence* to the *Niagara* during the Battle of Lake Erie in September 1813.

When Commodore Oliver Perry complained of the "motley [mixed in color] set" of men sent to his squadron, Commodore Isaac Chauncey replied angrily, "I have yet to learn that the color of the skin . . . can effect a man's qualifications or usefulness. I have nearly fifty blacks aboard this ship, and many of them are among my best men." African Americans also did service aboard privateers.

Unlike the U.S Navy, the U.S. Army did not regularly enlist African Americans. When the crews of blockaded ships were used to reinforce army troops, however, some blacks took part in land battles. Much of Joshua Barney's crew, which fought valiantly at Bladensburg, Maryland, in August 1814 to protect Washington, D.C., was African American. At Plattsburgh, on the other hand, African American sailors were organized into a segregated regiment and assigned to dig trenches. One of these sailors, Charles Black, volunteered as an oarsman on Macdonough's gunboats. Having been impressed and imprisoned in England, he was eager to fight the British.

Andrew Jackson was the only U.S. general to welcome African Americans to military service. In preparing for the Battle of New Orleans, he organized a battalion of free blacks, whom he called "brave fellow citizens" and paid them the same amount as white soldiers. The British also recruited blacks for the assault on New Orleans. Besides bringing West Indian troops from Jamaica, the British appealed to runaway slaves. About 300 entered British service before the battle, and hundreds more joined as the British withdrew after the battle.

An African American soldier (*right of center*) reloads his musket during the Battle of New Orleans in January 1815.

A NIGHT BATTLE

The British soon retreated to Fort George on Lake Ontario, where more troops arrived, doubling the number of the British forces on the Niagara frontier. Leading this army was the commander in chief of Upper Canada, Lieutenant General Gordon Drummond. Because they lacked the heavy guns needed to challenge Fort George, U.S. general Jacob Brown's troops remained at Chippewa and Fort Erie.

On July 25, Brown heard that Drummond was planning to capture U.S. bases on the New York side of the Niagara and sent General Winfield Scott to stop the British from crossing the Niagara River.

Drummond, however, was marching toward Lundy's Lane, just three miles north of Chippewa.

That afternoon, as Scott came around a bend in the road, he saw the redcoats lined up at the top of a ridge beyond a patchwork of open fields. A battery of five guns immediately opened fire. Cannonballs, grapeshot, and musket balls flew down as Scott's men formed three battalions and set up their artillery. For two hours, the Americans struggled forward.

Brown arrived at nine o'clock, as light was fading, and sent fresh troops onto the battlefield. At the same time, Drummond also received additional men and guns.

In the nighttime battle at Lundy's Lane, Colonel James Miller led the assault on the seven heavy British cannons firing down on U.S. troops.

"I'll Try, Sir!"

A powerful battery of seven heavy guns pounded down on the Americans as they struggled up the slope toward the British line at Lundy's Lane. Seizing the guns was essential to winning the battle. When Major General Jacob Brown ordered Colonel James Miller to take his regiment and storm the guns, Miller replied, "I'll try, sir!" After his courageous assault on the battery succeeded in turning the tide of the battle, Miller's modest answer became the motto of his regiment.

Realizing that the artillery on the ridge was the key to the battle, Brown sent men to attack it by stealth. Creeping up along a fence covered with shrubbery, aided by the falling darkness, the men fired a deadly volley at the artillerymen as they lit their matches.

At 10:30 the Americans lined what remained of their troops and guns along the crest and waited in the darkness for the British counterattack. Drummond's men marched forward. Someone started firing, and for 20 minutes, both sides aimed at the flashes of fire from each other's muskets. The troops were so close together, one soldier said later, that "the continual blaze of light was such as to enable us distinctly to see their buttons."

The British retreated and attacked twice more. During each lull, the Americans prepared for the next assault, removing bullets from the dead and wounded for ammunition and consolidating their line. On the third attack, both Scott and Brown were seriously wounded. The British, however, did not return again. At midnight the exhausted and thirsty Americans held the field.

It was the largest and hardest-fought battle of the war up to that time. Both sides claimed victory. Although the Americans won the battle, they gained no territory or advantage over the enemy. The British, on the other hand, had stymied the invasion. On July 27, Brown's army moved back to Fort Erie. In spite of their two victories, the Americans held only the same 15 acres of Canada that they had captured on July 3.

THE SIEGE OF FORT ERIE

The Americans spent the next two weeks strengthening Fort Erie. They installed new batteries, added walls, mounded dirt to protect the campsite, dug ditches, and chopped down trees to build an abatis (an obstacle of sharpened tree branches facing the enemy.) The British set up camp a mile to the north and, bringing their guns to the edge of the Niagara River, aimed them at the fort.

A Trapped Deserter

The Americans who built the abatis at Fort Erie did not just use trees with sharpened branches. They added briers (thorny stems) to the pile. One night a deserter from the British army tried to cross the abatis. Becoming hopelessly entangled, he cried out for help. After several hours, some Americans finally found and rescued him, but he lost most of his clothes to the thorns.

For two days, the British cannons bombarded the fort. Braced for an attack, one-third of the garrison patrolled all night. The rest slept in their clothes next to their weapons. At 2 A.M. on August 15, U.S. guards outside the fort heard the swishing of British troops stealing through wet woods toward the battery on Snake Hill at the southern end of the fort. The U.S. guards fired a warning signal and quickly retreated.

Atop Snake Hill, the Americans on the ramparts (broad, raised walkways) of the fort could make out the dark shapes of the British Forlorn Hope running toward the abatis with their bayonets set. The Americans opened fire with cannons and muskets. The British troops could not fire back. To ensure that no careless shots

EYEWITNESS QUOTE: EXPLOSION AT FORT ERIE

"Suddenly every sound was hushed by the sense of an unnatural tremor, beneath our feet, the first heave of an earthquake; and almost at the same instant, the center of the bastion [fortified area] burst up, with a terrific explosion and a jet of flame, mingled with fragments of timber, earth, stone, and bodies of men rose, to the height of one or two hundred feet, in the air, and fell, in a shower of ruins, to a great distance, all around."

—Second Lieutenant David Bates Douglass, U.S. Artillery, Fort Erie, August 15, 1814

gave away the surprise, the flints had been removed from their muskets.

Again and again, Drummond's troops tried to storm Snake Hill. After six desperate attempts, the much-depleted British troops retreated through the woods.

Meanwhile, a smaller British force stormed and captured a battery at the northern end of the fort. But before they could advance any farther, a tremendous explosion blew up the battery, ending the battle. The British survivors returned to their camp. The Americans had won the battle, but after six weeks of tough, often victorious fighting, they still held only one fort. They had to rebuild it and prepare to defend it again.

THE BRITISH
6 COUNTERATTACK

Bigger events soon overshadowed the quarrel over the Niagara frontier. Efforts to end the war had begun soon after war broke out. In October 1812, the Russian czar (ruler) offered to mediate between the United States and Britain. The United States accepted and sent delegates to Russia in May 1813. The same month, however, the British refused the Russian offer. In December 1813, the Americans learned that the British were willing to negotiate directly with the United States. For the next eight months, the two countries tried to agree on a site to hold the talks. At last, on August 8, 1814, U.S. and British negotiators sat down together in Ghent, Belgium, to begin hammering out a peace treaty.

To increase their power at the negotiating table, the British wanted to gain as much territory as possible. In the summer of 1814, the British launched a three-pronged assault on the United States: from Canada in the North, along the Atlantic coast, and up the Mississippi River from the Gulf of Mexico in the South. The British hoped to hold northern Maine, gain control of the Great Lakes, and stop U.S. expansion in the West.

WASHINGTON IN DANGER

British raids on the Atlantic coast, which had terrorized Americans during the summer of 1813, picked up again in 1814. In July President Madison appointed Brigadier General William

Washington in 1814

With fewer than 10,000 inhabitants, Washington, D.C., was still more of a village than a city. It had been the official capital of the United States for only 14 years. Hemmed in by swamps and woods, dusty in dry weather and muddy in wet, the small city was nevertheless elegantly laid out with broad avenues. The Capitol Building atop Capitol Hill had been completed just before the war. A mile away stood the president's residence (called the President's House), where President Madison's wife, Dolley, entertained visiting dignitaries in style.

Winder to raise and command a militia to defend Washington, D.C. The naval defenses, a fleet of gunboats, were entrusted to Commodore Joshua Barney.

On August 19, 4,500 British troops disembarked at Benedict, Maryland, about 30 miles southeast of Washington. Unopposed by any U.S. troops, they began marching in the stifling heat along the west bank of the Patuxent River. Accompanying the British was a squadron of armed boats led by Rear Admiral George Cockburn.

Upriver, Barney's flotilla was trapped. To prevent their capture by the British, Barney blew up his boats and marched his 400 sailors to Washington. General Winder, meanwhile, waited anxiously, not certain where to put his newly assembled militia. He expected the enemy to attack the city

from the east. Major General Robert Ross, the commander of the British ground troops, however, decided to march his army to Bladensburg, Maryland, where he could cross the shallow Anacostia River and approach Washington from the northeast.

At 10 A.M. on August 24, learning of Ross's new route, Winder ordered his men to join the 2,000 militiamen already at Bladensburg. President Madison, as well as most of his cabinet (advisers to the president), rode out to witness the battle.

THE BLADENSBURG RACES

On a hill outside Bladensburg, the Maryland militia watched two clouds of dust rising in the distance—the two armies racing toward them. At noon the Americans were still lining up across the hill on one side of the Anacostia River, when the redcoats, marching six abreast, came into view a mile away on the other side.

Even before all of their army had arrived, British troops began charging across the river. The Americans advanced and opened fire with cannons and muskets. The British kept coming. Those downed by U.S. fire were rapidly replaced by the men behind them. At first, the

William Winder *(left)* and **Joshua Barney** *(right)* helped defend Washington, D.C., against British attacks.

Americans held fast, and the redcoats took cover in the shrubbery along the riverbank.

Soon, however, the British had set up a weapon that was unfamiliar to many of the U.S. militiamen. Congreve rockets were a recent invention. They could lob a charge of metal balls up into the air and over a distance of two miles. A dozen or more rockets could be launched at one time, and they made a screaming noise as they shot upward. At the terrifying sound of the rockets and the sight of more redcoats splashing across the river, the untrained militia fled so fast that the battle came to be called the Bladensburg Races. "They ran like sheep, chased by dogs" wrote one of Barney's men later.

Barney and his sailors arrived after the battle had started and set up their artillery

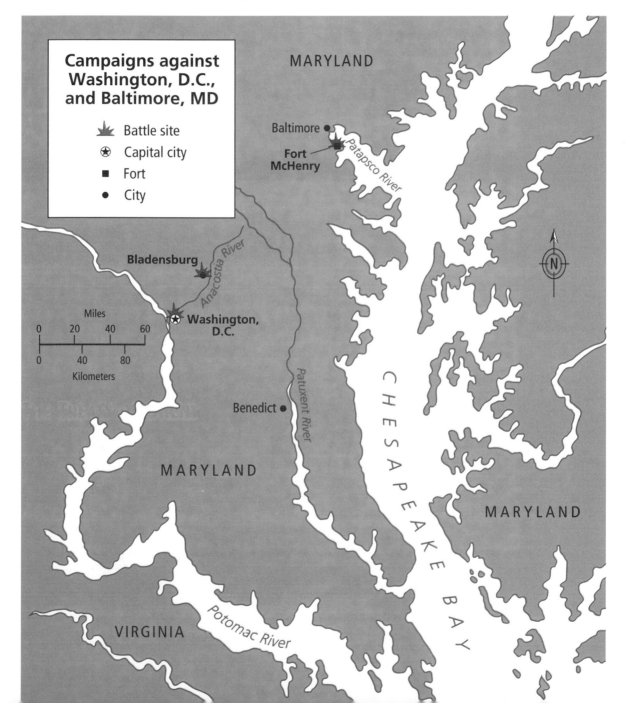

Campaigns against Washington, D.C., and Baltimore, MD

⚜ Battle site
✪ Capital city
■ Fort
● City

across the road. With a few hundred regular troops still fighting alongside them, Barney's gunners shelled the British until they ran out of ammunition. Barney, who was badly wounded, asked his officers to leave him in the field. When he was captured by the advancing British, they treated him with great respect for his bravery.

After the battle ended at 4 P.M., the British rested a few hours, marched to Washington unopposed, and set up camp just outside of town.

WASHINGTON IN FLAMES

While the two armies clashed at Bladensburg, Dolley Madison waited at the President's House, ready to leave at a moment's notice. She had loaded a carriage and a wagon with trunks full of important papers, books, silver, and the red velvet curtains from the President's House oval

drawing room. As she listened to the booming cannons, the first lady was also setting the table for 40 guests she hoped would arrive for dinner at 3 P.M. Instead, two messengers, covered with dust, galloped up to the house shouting "Clear out! Clear out! General Armstrong has ordered a retreat!"

Dolley Madison took time to rescue the large Gilbert Stuart portrait of George Washington from the dining room wall and a copy of the Declaration of Independence. She then joined the thousands of residents exiting the city.

When news of the rout (decisive defeat) in Bladensburg reached the commander of the Washington Navy Yard, he lit fuses set earlier in the day to prevent the British from capturing the naval stores and ships. Sheds and workshops full of ropes and sailcloth, stacks of timber, and a variety of boats fueled the blaze. The spreading flames set off loud explosions as they reached stockpiles of ammunition. It was the first of many fires in Washington that day.

When the British entered the city toward nightfall, they piled mahogany desks, tables, and chairs into a bonfire inside the Capitol. Flames raced up curtains to the wooden flooring and seats of the public galleries. The intense heat melted glass lamps. On the western end of the building, 3,000 books of the Library of Congress were consumed. The roof collapsed, leaving only the massive outer walls standing.

Dolley Madison was able to take the painting of George Washington and a copy of the Declaration Independence with her when she fled Washington ahead of the British.

British troops entered Washington, D.C., and set fire to many buildings.

Cockburn and Ross then led troops down the tree-lined avenue to the President's House. After toasting their victory with Madison's wine, the men pushed hand-carved gilded chairs, red velvet cushions, sofas, and tables together and torched the piles. Fire rushed through the mansion until smoke and flames burst through the roof. While the arsonists moved on to nearby government offices, Cockburn, Ross, and other officers enjoyed dinner at a boardinghouse. Cockburn blew out the candles lighting their meal, saying he preferred to dine by the fiery glow of burning Washington. The next day, the British continued destroying public buildings, setting fire to the State and War Department offices. That evening, after an 8 P.M. curfew sent everyone indoors, the British troops quietly left the city and marched back to their ships.

Cockburn's Revenge

Among the buildings that the British wrecked in Washington were the offices of the *National Intelligencer,* a pro-war newspaper that frequently made fun of British leaders in sharply negative language. Admiral Cockburn personally supervised the troops as they heaped newspapers, furniture, books, and papers into a bonfire and dumped the lead printing type on top. "Be sure that all the C's are destroyed," he told his men, "so that the rascals cannot any longer abuse my name."

FAST FACT

JEFFERSON'S BOOKS

After the burning of Washington, Thomas Jefferson offered his own personal library of 7,000 volumes to replace the books in the Library of Congress that were lost in the fire. Congress voted to pay him $23,950 for the books, which became the basis of the largest library in the United States.

WOMEN IN THE WAR OF 1812

Women's roles in the War of 1812 were strictly behind the scenes but no less important to the war effort. Rarely mentioned in the official reports and accounts, the wives of officers and enlisted men helped out in forts and on ships. Besides helping with laundry, mending, cooking, and cleaning, they tended the sick and wrote letters for the men. In the British army, wives of enlisted men drew lots to determine who would travel with the army, with one woman keeping house for every 10 men. Their duties included fetching water and setting up and striking camp.

One heroine was a wife aboard the *Confiance*, the British flagship during the Battle of Plattsburgh. She was binding up a seaman's wounds with fabric she tore from her skirt when she was struck in the chest by a cannonball. Had she not been killed in the battle, it is unlikely that anyone would have recorded her presence on the ship.

On the U.S. side at the same battle, General Alexander Macomb was so short of men that when Commodore Thomas Macdonough requested oarsmen for his gunboats, he asked his military band members for volunteers. The wife of a musician stepped forward and served as an oarsman in the battle.

It is possible that a few women served in the military disguised as men. But a book published in 1815 that claims to be an account of Lucy Brewer's life as a marine aboard the *Constitution* has proved to be entirely fictional.

On the home front, women formed committees to help the war effort. In New Orleans, women established hospitals and donated sheets, lint (for packing wounds), and clothing. When the Kentucky militia arrived in rags, the women sewed 1,200 cloaks, 275 vests, 1,127 pairs of pants, 800 shirts, 410 pairs of shoes, and a large number of mattresses in one week.

The U.S. woman most remembered for her role in the war is Dolley Madison. By keeping calm during the panic that seized Washington after the rout at Bladensburg, she saved national treasures that would otherwise have gone up in flames.

A soldier's wife loads cannonballs into a furnace to prepare hot shot during the War of 1812.

INVASION FROM THE NORTH

While U.S. attention was riveted on the capital, thousands of British soldiers were gathering near Montreal to invade the United States. At the British shipyard on Isle aux Noix, shipwrights had built a frigate, the *Confiance,* that was larger, faster, and better-armed than any U.S. ship on Lake Champlain.

On September 1, while carpenters and riggers prepared the *Confiance* for battle, the British infantry marched into northern New York State. Panicky residents packed up and left. The militia from six New York counties quickly gathered, and calls were sent to Vermont for more. Militiamen shot at the redcoats from the woods, but the British did not stop to engage in battle. They simply marched on through the late summer heat as their skirmishers chased off the militiamen like pesky insects.

The same day, U.S. Navy commodore Thomas Macdonough brought his

Thomas Macdonough

Lake Champlain fleet into Plattsburgh Bay. Knowing that the British fleet had more long-range guns than he did, he wanted to avoid a battle on the open lake. Inside the narrow bay, his powerful carronades could reach the enemy. The winds needed to bring the British fleet south would make the U-turn into the bay a tricky maneuver, giving the Americans the opportunity to fire first.

Macdonough anchored his four ships, the *Eagle,* the flagship *Saratoga,* the *Ticonderoga,* and the *Preble,* across the entrance to the bay. Ten gunboats guarded gaps between the ships. He arranged a series of anchors and ropes so that he would be able to turn his ships around during the battle if he needed to.

In Plattsburgh, U.S. Army brigadier general Alexander Macomb refused to retreat. "The eyes of America are on us," he told his men. "Fortune always favors the brave." With a fighting force of only 1,770 men, he prepared to make a stand at three earthen forts on the south side of the Saranac River, which cuts through the village of Plattsburgh before emptying into Lake Champlain. He set up a hospital on Crab Island in the bay. The strongest invalids took charge of a battery of guns.

When the British marched into town on September 6, they found the north side of town deserted and no boards on the two bridges across the Saranac. Blockhouses guarded the lower bridge and the lakefront. While the British waited for naval support, militia from Vermont and

Phantom Forces

Eleazer Williams, a scout for the American army, crossed Lake Champlain to Vermont. He obtained an official letter saying, falsely, that the governor of Vermont was on his way to Plattsburgh with 10,000 men and that 9,000 more were due from other Vermont counties. He then recrossed the lake to the British camp and let the letter fall into British hands. The British army fled.

Comparing Naval Power

In estimating naval strength, the size and range of the guns play an important role. The firepower of a particular ship or fleet is determined by multiplying the weight of the cannonballs by the number of guns that fire them and adding up all results.

The *Saratoga* carried eight 24-pound guns (8 x 24 = 192), six 42-pound guns (6 x 42 = 252), and twelve 32-pound guns (12 x 32 = 384). Her total firepower would be 828 pounds. Usually, however, only one side of a ship is engaged at any one time in a battle. To calculate her "broadside" strength, you need to add up the guns on one side of the ship together with the power of any stern (back) or bow (front) guns that can be turned to either side. The *Saratoga* could throw 414 pounds of metal with each broadside. The *Confiance*, with the same number of guns, could throw 480 pounds in a broadside.

The range of the guns also played a role in naval battles. The *Saratoga* could only throw 96 pounds of metal at long range but could hammer out 318 pounds at close range. At a distance, the *Confiance*, with many more long-range guns, could send out 384 pounds of metal. Macdonough's strategy of getting the British fleet into the bay where he could use his short-range guns was crucial to defeating the British fleet.

New York, as well as seamen from ships blockaded in Boston Harbor, arrived to bolster Macomb's forces.

THE BATTLE ON LAKE CHAMPLAIN

Early on September 11, the British ships—the *Chub,* the *Linnet,* the *Confiance,* and the *Finch*—and 12 gunboats sailed into Plattsburgh Bay. Just as Macdonough planned, the *Saratoga* fired at the *Confiance*

A Good Omen

The first shot to strike a ship at the Battle of Plattsburgh hit a chicken coop on the deck of the *Saratoga*. A rooster that had been penned inside flew into the rigging and crowed lustily. The crew cheered. It seemed a good omen at the start of the battle.

with its long cannon as it headed toward the U.S. line. The ball tore down the deck, destroying the ship's wheel and killing and wounding the men in its path. While the British struggled against the wind to position their ships for the fight, the Americans pounded them with their long guns.

Although wounded, the *Confiance* turned and dropped anchor 300 yards away from the *Saratoga*. The *Confiance* opened fire with a well-aimed broadside. The British ships had double-loaded their guns for their first round, so that two balls flew out of each of the *Confiance*'s 18 cannons on its port (left) side.

Smoke and deafening booms filled the air. The British *Chub* was soon disabled by the *Eagle*'s carronades. On board the *Confiance,* the British commandant, George Downie, was standing behind a long cannon when a ball shot from the *Saratoga* struck its muzzle. The cannon slammed into the British captain, instantly killing him.

Meanwhile, Macdonough had his hands full. Both the *Confiance,* with 37 guns, and the 18-gun *Linnet* were firing at his 26-gun flagship. The *Confiance* was equipped with a furnace for heating cannonballs. Twice, hot shot started fires aboard the *Saratoga,* which the crew rushed to put out.

The *Finch,* battered by the *Ticonderoga,* lost control and veered south toward Crab Island, where it hit shallow water. Menaced by the guns operated by the hospital

EYEWITNESS QUOTE:
THE LAKE BATTLE

"The firing was terrific, fairly shaking the ground, and so rapid that it seemed to be one continuous roar, intermingled with spiteful flashing from the mouths of the guns, and dense clouds of smoke soon hung over the two fleets."

—Julius Hubbell, U.S. civilian who witnessed the Battle of Plattsburgh, 1814

patients on the island, the *Finch* surrendered. The *Preble,* threatened with boarding by four British gunboats, each with more men than the *Preble* had left, pulled away from the battle to the protection of the U.S. batteries onshore.

The five remaining ships had few working guns left on their engaged sides. This is when Macdonough's preparations had paid off. He cut off some of the anchor lines holding the *Saratoga* in place and pulled in others to turn the ship around 180 degrees. This maneuver gave Macdonough a dozen fresh guns on the other side of the ship to train

Commodore Thomas Macdonough's careful planning led to a U.S. victory on Lake Champlain.

on the ailing *Confiance*. When the *Saratoga* renewed its assault, the British lowered their flag in surrender.

In two and one-half hours, all of the British ships had been pounded into wrecks. The brand-new *Confiance* had 105 cannonball holes in its hull. One sailor remarked that its masts looked like "bunches of matches" and its sails like "a bundle of rags."

THE BRITISH RETREAT

When the lake battle began, the British batteries opened fire on the forts across the Saranac River commanded by General Macomb. The heavy bombardment of cannonballs, shrapnel, bombshells, and Congreve rockets soon crippled the guns of the closest U.S. blockhouse.

The British infantry began their assault an hour later. One brigade stormed the two bridges in town, but the steady fire of Macomb's men repeatedly drove them back.

The other two brigades were sent through the woods to cross the Saranac at a ford (shallow crossing) three miles

upstream, but they became lost in a maze of tracks that Macomb's troops had prepared before the battle. When the British brigades finally reached the ford, Vermont militiamen hidden on the opposite bank peppered them with musket fire as the British waded into the swift stream. The redcoats could not be stopped, however. As more and more British soldiers crossed the river, the militia scattered. The brigades were preparing to attack Macomb's flank (the side of a formation) when a message arrived from Prevost announcing the defeat of the British fleet and ordering a retreat.

The British invasion had been repelled. Americans across the country celebrated with bonfires and fireworks.

THE BOMBARDMENT OF BALTIMORE

While Britain's invasion force was occupying Plattsburgh, Admiral Cochrane's British forces in the Chesapeake were taking aim at a new target—Baltimore. This prosperous port was the third largest city in the United States. Admiral Cochrane

It looked as if the British were going to overrun U.S. defenses in Plattsburgh, but after the American victory on Lake Champlain, the British were ordered to retreat.

British Congreve rockets and bomb ships bombarded Fort McHenry near Baltimore through the night of September 13, 1814. Finally, in the morning, the British called off the unsuccessful attack.

wanted to punish the city for sending out so many privateers to harass British shipping. Baltimore was "a nest of pirates," he said, which "ought to be laid in ashes." The British expected to find the city as poorly defended as Washington had been two and one-half weeks earlier.

The destructive attack on the nation's capital, however, had caused a surge of patriotism. Volunteers poured into Baltimore to build defenses. The mayor and the citizens pitched in as well, digging trenches and constructing a defensive wall with openings from which U.S. troops could fire on an approaching army. Gunners from blockaded U.S. ships arrived to take charge of the cannons.

The imposing, star-shaped Fort McHenry protected the harbor entrance. Major George Armistead commanded a force of 1,000 men and 57 heavy guns ready to stop British ships from reaching the city.

British troops disembarked at the mouth of the Patapsco River early on September 12 and began the 17-mile march to Baltimore. Maryland militia, sent out from the city to confront the redcoats on North Point Peninsula, were unable to stop the advancing troops. Meanwhile, 17 British warships headed up the Patapsco River toward the harbor.

September 13 dawned with the hissing of rockets arcing high through the haze over the Patapsco River. Two miles below Fort McHenry, Cochrane's British fleet had formed its battle lines. Soon five bomb ships began slamming shells into the sturdy fort. When the Americans fired back, however, their ammunition fell short.

All day the British kept up a steady bombardment, hour after hour, firing on average a shell or bomb a minute. During the afternoon, one shell exploded on the walls of the fort, killing two men and

The Star-Spangled Banner

On a British ship a few miles behind the vessels bombarding Fort McHenry, three Americans watched in suspense. One, a Maryland doctor who had arrested some British soldiers retreating from Washington, was being held as a prisoner of war by the British. The others were a U.S. agent for prisoner exchange and Francis Scott Key, a Washington lawyer, who had come to negotiate the doctor's release. Cochrane had agreed to free the doctor, but he put the three Americans under guard until after the battle.

All night the men listened to the guns. So long as the guns were firing, they knew that the fort had not been taken. A pause in the bombardment just before dawn, however, filled them with dread. When daylight broke, they saw the stars and stripes of the U.S. flag waving above the fort.

Filled with patriotic pride, Key scribbled a poem describing his nighttime fears and the thrill of victory symbolized by the "star-spangled banner" atop the fort. He set it to the music of a popular English song, "To Anacreon in Heaven." When he reached Baltimore on the evening of September 16, he had the song printed on a handbill and distributed around the city.

The new song caught on quickly. On March 3, 1931, the "Star-Spangled Banner" officially become the national anthem of the United States.

Frances Scott Key (standing) **watches the bombardment of Fort McHenry from a British ship.**

wounding four others. Seeing their success, three bomb ships moved closer, only to backtrack when every cannon and mortar in the fort fired on them.

That evening, the entire sky was lit up by the constant shelling. The British army arrived outside Baltimore after a difficult march over barricaded roads. Cochrane, however, realized that his ships would never be able to get past Fort McHenry to support the land troops, and

he called off the attack. At 3 A.M., the weary British troops turned around and began moving out along the road they had just come in on.

To cover the British retreat, Cochrane continued his bombardment through the night. Finally, in the morning, 25 hours and an estimated 1,500 to 1,800 rounds of ammunition after it began, the bombing ended. Major Armistead hoisted a large U.S. flag in celebration.

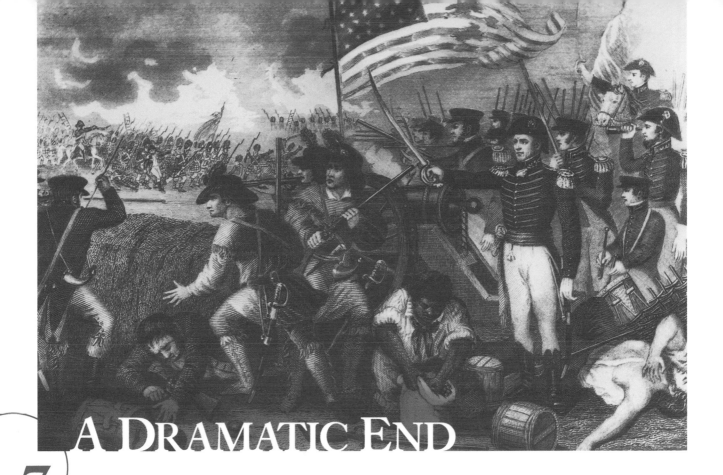

A DRAMATIC END

7

Although the victories in Plattsburgh and Baltimore cheered Americans, the war was not yet over. In Ghent the U.S. negotiators, John Quincy Adams, Henry Clay, Albert Gallatin, James Bayard, and Jonathan Russell, were considering the demands of the British peace commission. The British refused outright to include in a peace treaty any mention of impressment or blockades—the issues that had caused the United States to declare war. Instead, the British wanted the United States to grant about 250,000 square miles of U.S. territory to Native Americans, give up fishing rights in Canadian waters, grant Britain free access to the Mississippi River, hand over northern Maine, and remove warships and forts from the Great Lakes.

The U.S. commissioners firmly opposed all of the British demands. Little by little, the British began backing down. The U.S. victories in Plattsburgh and Baltimore helped. By October the British had dropped their demands for Native American lands. Instead, they asked to keep territory they had won in the war. The Americans refused. The British, however, still hoped that a decisive victory in New Orleans would improve their chances of gaining a favorable treaty.

THE BRITISH ADVANCE ON NEW ORLEANS

On December 1, General Andrew Jackson arrived in New Orleans after his successes in the Creek War and began preparing for the city's defense. Five gunboats were sent

A Beautiful City

New Orleans in 1814 was a beautiful city. Brick houses with graceful ironwork balconies and courtyard gardens full of tropical flowers faced the straight, wide streets. Founded by French settlers in 1718, the city became part of the United States of America in 1803, when President Thomas Jefferson purchased Louisiana from France. Most of New Orleans's 25,000 citizens spoke French, not English.

The city was also wealthy. Warehouses crammed with cotton, sugar, and rice lined the Mississippi River waterfront. Fertile plantations along the river grew fruits and vegetables and raised livestock. Farmers, fur trappers, and lumbermen living farther north on the Mississippi and its many tributaries shipped goods to the city. Oceangoing ships brought luxury goods from abroad. By capturing New Orleans, the British could gain control over all this trade.

to patrol Lake Borgne, a shallow lake east of the city that opens into the Gulf of Mexico. Forts all around the city were reinforced. Bayous, the creeks that wandered through the cypress swamps between the lakes and the city, were blocked with downed trees. But Jackson did not have enough men and supplies and had very little time.

On December 12, the British fleet anchored near Cat Island at the entrance to the lake, about 70 miles from New Orleans. Two days later, a flotilla of 45 armed barges carrying more than 1,000 British marines and seamen rowed into Lake Borgne and captured the five U.S. gunboats.

Hearing news of the loss, Jackson sent orders to officers outside the city to rush their men to New Orleans. Jackson even accepted help from pirates Jean Laffite and Dominique You, whose offer of men, weapons, and ammunition Jackson had earlier refused.

With Lake Borgne undefended, the British began ferrying troops to a small deserted island at the northern end of the

The British fleet moved into Lake Borgne, east of New Orleans, and captured five U.S. gunboats.

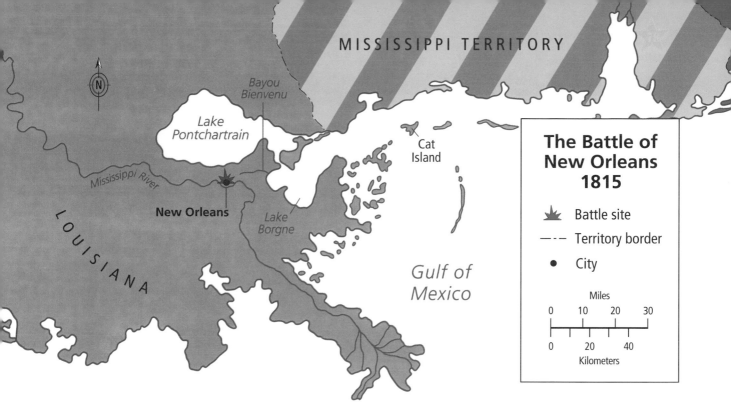

The Battle of
New Orleans
1815

⚜ Battle site
--- Territory border
● City

Miles
0 10 20 30

0 20 40
Kilometers

lake. From there they rowed into unblocked Bayou Bienvenu that led to a plantation on the Mississippi River several miles south of New Orleans. Late in the morning on December 23, Major Gabriel Villeré was relaxing on the porch of his father's plantation. Spotting red uniforms darting through an orange grove, he rushed to New Orleans to warn Jackson.

Jackson raised the alarm and gathered 1,800 men for a night attack. About a mile above the British camp, he formed his lines so quietly that not even the British sentries 500 yards away suspected they were there. Then the Americans waited for the signal from the *Carolina*, which had sailed down the Mississippi to bombard the British camp with its guns.

At 7:30 P.M., the exhausted British troops were feasting on food taken from nearby plantations and preparing to sleep, when the *Carolina* opened fire. The British had no sooner huddled under the high riverbank to escape the deadly shot from the schooner than Jackson's army burst on them with loud yells and blazing muskets. In darkness and fog, with brief intervals of moonlight, the two sides fought at close range with swords, bayonets, tomahawks, and hunting knives. At about 9:30, Jackson withdrew to his original position, having shown the British that they were up against a determined foe.

EYEWITNESS QUOTE:
JACKSON ATTACKS

"Flash, flash, flash came from the river; the roar of the cannon followed, and the light of her own broadside displayed to us an enemy's vessel at anchor near the opposite bank, and pouring a perfect shower of grape and round shot, into the camp."

—George Gleig,
British officer,
Villeré plantation,
December 23, 1814

THE ENEMY'S POINT OF VIEW

Great Britain viewed the United States not so much as an enemy but as an annoying young child who was throwing tantrums. These tantrums were getting in the way of the really important business of rescuing Europe from Napoleon, whose dreams of empire threatened the independence of every European nation.

The issues that riled Americans were the direct result of Britain's war against France. To protect the British Isles from invasion, Britain needed a strong navy. Britain felt it had the right to impress seamen and to reclaim deserters from the Royal Navy who signed on U.S. naval or merchant ships. Britain also believed that native-born Englishmen had no right to change their nationality and become Americans to escape serving in the army or navy. Furthermore, by trading with France, the British maintained, the United States was giving aid to their enemy. Many Britons even believed that the United States sided with Napoleon.

Most Canadians agreed. A statement issued by the Assembly of Upper Canada in August 1812 declared that it was Great Britain, not the United States, "which contends for the relief of oppressed nations, the last pillar of true liberty, and the last refuge of afflicted humanity." A French-Canadian newspaper compared Americans to Goths and Vandals, people of northern tribes who had overcome the Roman Empire centuries earlier.

Many Canadians had fled the United States during and after the Revolutionary War because they believed that American democracy was a political experiment that was doomed to failure. Elected officials, they argued, would have to spend more time trying to please voters than governing the nation. Party politics would become more important than the well-being of the people. They pointed to the French Revolution and its aftermath—mob rule and a government headed by the despot Napoleon—to predict the future of the United States. Immigration from many parts of Europe, they felt, only increased the chances that democracy would fail.

In the spring of 1814, as the British celebrated their victory over Napoleon, their resentment of what they considered U.S. support of the enemy increased. It was time to punish the Americans. A London newspaper reflected popular feeling when the editors wrote of the need to "chastise the savages." A similar attitude was expressed by Vice Admiral Alexander Cochrane. In a letter to Lord Allen Bathurst, the British secretary for war, Cochrane said that he was eager to give the Americans "a complete drubbing [decisive defeat] before peace is made."

AN ARTILLERY BATTLE

After the battle, Jackson began constructing breastworks two miles north of the British camp, at the narrowest point between the Mississippi and the cypress swamp. "Here we shall plant our stakes," Jackson declared. "and not abandon them until we drive these red-coated rascals into the river, or the swamp."

Over the next few days, the Americans badgered the British with sniper fire and cannonades from the *Louisiana* and *Carolina* on the river. Mounted riflemen patrolled the area between the camps to keep British scouts from observing Jackson's position.

More British troops arrived, among them Sir Edward Pakenham, the British commanding general, ready to lead the offensive. After destroying the *Carolina* and chasing off the *Louisiana,* the British advanced toward the city on December 28. Passing a bend in the road, they discovered Jackson's defenses, studded with cannons pointed directly at them. The troops quickly took battle formations and brought up their artillery, but they could do little against the U.S. cannonade. To prevent further losses, Pakenham ordered a retreat and sent for more cannons from his ships.

The night of December 31, the British secretly dragged their guns toward the U.S. line. Three hundred yards from Jackson's breastworks, the British built six batteries using barrels full of sugar from the store-houses of neighboring plantations to make protective walls for their gunners.

The next morning, Jackson's troops were preparing to celebrate the new year with a military review. At 10 A.M., the fog lifted to reveal the British guns. The Americans scrambled to their positions as cannonballs flew overhead.

For three hours, the guns shook the ground as they belched their deadly missiles. The British had more and larger cannons than the Americans, firing 300 pounds of metal with each salvo (a firing of two guns simultaneously), compared to only 224 pounds from the Americans.

As they moved toward New Orleans, British troops found Jackson's forces facing them behind U.S. breastworks (*right*).

Nevertheless, when the firing let up and the smoke cleared, the Americans could see that their guns had caused more damage. The British batteries were demolished, several guns smashed, the sugar barrels shattered, and many gunners killed. The Americans had aimed more carefully and fired more rapidly. Most of the U.S. casualties were not soldiers at all, but civilians who had come to watch the battle and were standing behind the U.S. lines.

THE BATTLE OF NEW ORLEANS

For a week, both sides waited for reinforcements. Jackson's men kept working on their defenses and checking for British movement north of the city. Two thousand Kentuckians arrived on January 3.

The British spent the week digging a canal through the swampland between the bayou and the river. They hoped to

> ### Unusual Kentuckians
>
> A battalion of Kentuckians arrived to help defend New Orleans in January 1815, but they brought no guns with them. On hearing that the men had no firearms, Jackson said, "I don't believe it. I have never seen a Kentuckian without a gun and a pack of cards and a bottle of whiskey in my life."

bring in boats so that 1,400 men could cross the river, capture U.S. batteries there, and turn them on Jackson's defenses. Jackson found out about the plan and ordered 400 Kentuckians—all he could spare—to join the Louisiana militia guarding the batteries.

At 8 A.M. on January 8, when the early fog cleared, Americans guarding the breastworks saw a wave of redcoats charging toward them. As soon as the British got

This bird's-eye view of the Battle of New Orleans is from a sketch by General Jackson's chief engineer.

within 500 yards, the American artillery opened fire. Grapeshot and canister cut ragged holes in the rushing columns of men. At 300 yards, the American sharpshooters joined in with deadly rifle fire. By the time the British reached musket range, at 100 yards, their ranks were already seriously thinned.

An American later wrote that "the atmosphere was filled with sheets of fire, and volumes of smoke." A British officer who had earlier fought in Europe against Napoleon said that the fire "was the most murderous I ever beheld before or since." Pakenham and his second in command were both killed as they rallied their troops. Other officers were seriously wounded. Their men fled or dropped to the ground for safety.

Only 350 British troops had crossed the river. By the time they chased the militia away from the batteries, it was too late to use the guns to support the attack on Jackson's line. Long before then, the new British commander, General John Lambert, had ordered a retreat. The Battle of New Orleans, the largest and most uneven battle of the war, was over.

THE TREATY OF GHENT

The victory in New Orleans on January 8, 1815, was the last major engagement of the War of 1812. What the combatants did not know as they fought that bloody and decisive battle was that the war was over. On Christmas Eve 1814, the peace negotiators in Ghent, Belgium, had agreed on a treaty.

In mid-November, the Americans had proposed a return to the boundaries that were in place before the war. By then both

sides were eager for the war to end. Britain faced problems in Europe, where many issues needed to be resolved after the defeat of Napoleon. The British people were also protesting further taxation to support the expense of the war in America. The cost of the war had also pushed the United States close to bankruptcy. Opposition to the war had increased to the point that some New Englanders wanted to separate from the United States. A return to the status quo was the simplest solution for ending the hostilities.

The ship carrying copies of the treaty arrived in New York on February 11, 1815. After being approved by Congress, the treaty took effect on February 17.

In the United States, New England opponents of the war declared that the Treaty of Ghent only proved the uselessness of two and one-half years of fighting. But the southerners hailed it as a victory. "We have stood the contest, singlehanded, against the conqueror of Europe," crowed a southern judge. Americans across the nation celebrated the peace with fireworks and thanksgiving services. To many Americans, the war was a triumph over Britain, a second war of independence, even more glorious than the first.

EPILOGUE

The War of 1812 brought no major changes in territory. However, it had a significant impact on the United States and on U.S. relations with Great Britain and other foreign states.

The Treaty of Ghent required commissions to resolve disputes along the United States–Canada border, which were settled over the next few years. The pattern was set for resolving problems through diplomatic negotiation instead of war.

For Canada, the war united the mix of French, British, Native American, and U.S. settlers. Instead of joining the Americans, most Canadians realized that they preferred the security of British rule to U.S. democracy. A new Canadian nationalism (loyalty and devotedness to a nation), based on loyalty to Britain, developed as a result of the war.

The economic impact of the blockades before and during the war led to a growth of industry in the United States. New England textile mills freed Americans from dependence on imported British cloth. After the war, manufacturing plants that used waterpower to drive machinery developed along rivers in the Northeast.

Although the treaty left out mention of impressment, Americans argued that ships at sea were under the authority of the country from which they came. This argument influenced the development of international maritime (naval) laws.

The United States learned from the experience that to gain international respect, a nation needs to be prepared to defend its rights. Realizing that military preparedness is essential even in times of peace, the United States never again let its army grow smaller as it had after the Revolutionary War.

The British efforts at blocking the U.S. expansion westward failed, and the United States resumed its rapid growth after the war. The real losers in the war were the Native Americans. Many had hoped that by supporting the British, they could prevent settlers from taking over Native American hunting grounds and maybe even regain land sold before the war. The loss of Tecumseh at the Battle of the Thames River in the North and the defeat of the Creek at the Battle of Horseshoe Bend in the South weakened Native American resistance to U.S. settlement.

Westward expansion also opened up new territories for slavery. Both the British and the Americans had abolished the international slave trade and agreed in the Treaty of Ghent to stop slave trading within their countries. Yet slavery spread as U.S. slaveholders moved westward. Slavery later became a major issue dividing Americans. Finally, U.S. pride in having defeated the most powerful army and navy in the world stirred up a new nationalism that helped to bond the growing nation for almost 50 years.

MAJOR BATTLES OF THE WAR OF 1812

USS *Constitution* vs. HMS *Guerrière*	**August 19, 1812**
Queenston, Canada	**October 13, 1812**
USS *United States* vs. HMS *Macedonian* (Madeira, off the west coast of Africa)	**October 25, 1812**
Raisin River, Monroe, MI	**January 21, 1813**
Fort York, Canada	**April 27, 1813**
Fort Meigs, Perrysburg, OH	**May 5, 1813**
Fort George, Canada	**May 27, 1813**
Sackets Harbor, NY	**May 29, 1813**
USS *Chesapeake* vs. HMS *Shannon*	**June 1, 1813**
Fort Mims, AL	**August 30, 1813**
Lake Erie, PA	**September 10, 1813**
Thames River, Canada	**October 5, 1813**
Horseshoe Bend, AL	**March 27, 1814**
Chippewa, Canada	**July 5, 1814**
Lundy's Lane, Canada	**July 25, 1814**
Fort Erie, Canada	**August 15, 1814**
Bladensburg, MD	**August 25, 1814**
Plattsburgh, NY (Lake Champlain)	**September 11, 1814**
Fort McHenry, MD	**September 13–14, 1814**
New Orleans, LA	**January 8, 1815**

Lake Superior

CANADA
(GREAT BRITAIN)

NEW HAMPSHIRE
VERMONT

Part of
MASSACHUSETTS

NEW
YORK

Fort
York

Lake Huron

Plattsburgh

USS *Constitution* vs.
HMS *Guerrière*

MICHIGAN
TERRITORY

Fort
George

Lake Ontario

Sackets
Harbor

USS *Chesapeake*
vs.
HMS *Shannon*

ILLINOIS
TERRITORY

Lake Michigan

Thames
River

Queenston
Lundy's Lane
Chippewa

MASSACHUSETTS

RHODE ISLAND

Raisin
River

Lake Erie

Fort Erie

CONNECTICUT

Fort
Meigs

Lake
Erie

PENNSYLVANIA

Fort
McHenry

NEW JERSEY

INDIANA
TERRITORY

OHIO

DELAWARE

MISSOURI
TERRITORY

Ohio River

Bladensburg

MARYLAND

VIRGINIA

ATLANTIC
OCEAN

KENTUCKY

NORTH
CAROLINA

Mississippi River

TENNESSEE

SOUTH
CAROLINA

Horseshoe
Bend

MISSISSIPPI
TERRITORY

GEORGIA

Fort
Mims

LOUISIANA

New Orleans

FLORIDA
(SPAIN)

Gulf of Mexico

Major Battles of the War of 1812

★ Major battle

State

U.S. territory

Other land

Miles
0   50 100 150 200

0   100   200   300
Kilometers

WAR OF 1812 TIMELINE

1807 HMS *Leopard* attacks and seizes men from USS *Chesapeake,* June 22.

1811 Battle of Tippecanoe fought on November 7.

1812 The United States declares war on Great Britain on June 18.

General Hull invades Canada, retreats, surrenders Detroit, July 12–August 16.

USS *Constitution* defeats HMS *Guerrière* on August 19.

Battle of Queenston is fought on October 13.

USS *United States* captures HMS *Macedonian* on October 25.

USS *Constitution* defeats HMS *Java* on December 29.

1813 U.S. soldiers massacred after the battle at the Raisin River, January 21.

Capture of York in Ontario, Canada, on April 27

Siege of Fort Meigs, May 1–9

HMS *Shannon* defeats USS *Chesapeake* on June 1.

Commodore Oliver Hazard Perry's ships defeat the British fleet on Lake Erie, September 10.

Tecumseh is killed at the Battle of the Thames River, October 5.

1814 The Creek Red Sticks are defeated at Horseshoe Bend on March 27.

U.S. troops capture Fort Erie, Canada, July 3.

British and U.S. troops fight the Battles of Chippewa (July 5) and Lundy's Lane (July 25).

British troops enter Washington, D.C., and burn the President's House, August 24–25.

The United States wins the naval battle on Lake Champlain and the land battle at Plattsburgh, September 11.

The British bombard Baltimore's Fort McHenry, September 13–14.

The Treaty of Ghent ends the war on December 24.

1815 Andrew Jackson leads U.S. troops to victory at the Battle of New Orleans, January 8.

Congress approves the Treaty of Ghent, February 17.

GLOSSARY

abatis a defensive obstacle built of downed trees with sharpened branches facing the enemy

artillery large, mounted firearms, such as howitzers and cannons, that are operated by a crew of gunners

battery a grouping of cannons, howitzers, and/or mortars placed at a strategic point to defend a fort, blockhouse, or line of battle

blockhouse a small building used for military defense, built of thick logs with loopholes in the sides for firing through, often with an upper story projecting out over the lower story

bow the front of a ship

breastworks a defensive wall

brig short for brigatine. A ship with two masts and sails hung across the width of the ship ("square-rigged sails")

broadside the firing of all the guns on one side of a ship in rapid succession

embargo an order by a government prohibiting commercial ships from leaving its ports

flagship the ship that carries the commander of the fleet and flies his flag

frigate a medium-sized warship with three masts and sails hung across the width of the ship ("square-rigged sails")

garrison a military post or the troops stationed at a military post

infantry soldiers trained, armed, and equipped to fight on foot

magazine a room in a fort or a ship where gunpowder and other explosives are stored

rampart a broad raised walkway or platform of earth or stone that is part of a fort and is usually next to a parapet, or wall, to protect soldiers

sanction an economic or military measure used to pressure a nation that is violating international law into complying with the law

schooner a ship with two masts and sails lined up along the length of the ship ("fore-and-aft sails")

ship of the line a warship large enough to have a place in the line of battle

skirmisher in the British army, a member of a flanking company (troops positioned to the right or left side of the central formation of troops) or light infantry (lightly armed foot soldiers) that patrolled the area around a military camp or march

sloop of war a small warship with guns on only one deck

stern the back of a ship

WHO'S WHO?

Isaac Brock (1769–1812)
The British general who outwitted General Hull at Detroit began his military career at 16 and served in the West Indies and Europe. Sent to Canada in 1802, he frequently asked to be transferred back to Europe, where he could win glory in battle. When war broke out in 1812, his quick offensive actions gained the support of the Indians and united Canadians, helping to prevent the loss of Canada to the United States.

Stephen Decatur Jr. (1779–1820)
In 1804 Stephen Decatur became a national hero after leading a daring mission to destroy a captured U.S. ship, the frigate *Philadelphia,* as she lay in the enemy's harbor at Tripoli. His success won him a promotion, making him at age 25, the youngest captain in U. S. naval history. His reputation soared again when, as captain of the *United States,* he defeated and captured the British ship *Macedonian* in 1812. Known for his short temper and combativeness, he died in a duel with Captain James Barron in 1820.

David Glasgow Farragut (1801–1870)
The famed Civil War hero got his start as a cabin boy aboard Captain David Porter's *Essex.* At one point during his cruise in the Pacific, Porter captured more ships than he had officers, so he put the 12-year-old Farragut in command of one of his prizes as the flotilla sailed into Valparaiso, Chile. When the *Essex* was finally defeated by two British naval vessels in March 1813, Farragut became a prisoner of war just like the other survivors.

Albert Gallatin (1761–1849)
Born in Geneva, Switzerland, Gallatin emigrated to the United States in 1780. A firm believer in U.S. democracy, he became involved in politics and served in Congress, where public finance became his main interest. Appointed secretary of the treasury by Jefferson and Madison, he tackled the difficult job of finding ways to pay for the war. In 1814 he played a major role in negotiating the Treaty of Ghent.

Jean Laffite (c. 1780–c.1826)
A Louisiana privateer and smuggler who preyed on Spanish ships in the Gulf of Mexico, Laffite turned down an offer from the British to aid them in capturing New Orleans. Instead, he sent information about British plans to U.S. general Jackson and provided him with crews for the *Carolina* and the *Louisiana,* and gunners, cannons, shot, and powder to defend the city. After the war, he returned to privateering.

Dolley Payne Madison (1768–1849)

Dolley Payne Todd was a widow with one son when she married Congressman James Madison in 1794. A vivacious woman known for her graciousness and charm, Dolley Madison soon became a popular hostess in Philadelphia and later in Washington when it became the new capital in 1800. When her husband was named secretary of state, she presided over social functions at the President's House for President Thomas Jefferson, who was a widower. In 1809 she became first lady.

Sir George Prevost (1767–1816)

Born in New Jersey, Sir George Prevost served in the British army in the West Indies and Nova Scotia before becoming the governor in chief and commander in chief of the British colonies in North America in 1812. His diplomatic abilities helped win the support of the French-Canadian community against the Americans. In war, however, he proved too cautious, withdrawing his troops too quickly from the attack on Sackets Harbor in 1813 and from Plattsburgh in 1814.

Winfield Scott (1786–1866)

One of the most accomplished soldiers in the U.S. Army before the Civil War, Scott began his military career in 1808. Six feet five inches tall, he was a commanding presence on the battlefield. Although forced to surrender at Queenston, he led the capture of Fort George in 1813 and Fort Erie in 1814 and the hard-fought victories at Chippewa and Lundy's Lane. His high standards of discipline, camp sanitation, dress, and military etiquette led to the nickname Old Fuss and Feathers. After the war, he reformed infantry tactics and led the invasion of central Mexico in the Mexican-American War (1846–1848).

Laura Ingersoll Secord (1775–1868)

Born in Massachusetts, Laura Ingersoll moved with her parents to Upper Canada as a child and married James Secord, another U.S. émigré. Her husband served in the Canadian militia during the war and was wounded at the Battle of Queenston. The following year, when the Americans captured Fort George, Laura Secord overheard U.S. soldiers discussing a plan to attack a British outpost at Beaver Dams. She set out on foot through woods on a 20-mile trek to warn the British, who ambushed the Americans. She became a national heroine to the Canadians.

Eleazer Derby Wood (1783–1814)

A skilled artillerist and engineer, Eleazer Wood supervised the building of Fort Meigs in northern Ohio and the expansion of Fort Erie in Ontario. "In the use of the axe, mattock and spade," he wrote, "consisted the chief military knowledge . . . and the salvation of the army." He was killed leading an attack to capture British cannons outside Fort Erie on September 17, 1814. A monument to his honor stands on the parade ground at West Point, and a fort was named for him in New York Harbor. This fort is the base for the Statue of Liberty.

SOURCE NOTES

5   Albert Marrin, *1812: The War Nobody Won* (New York: Atheneum, 1985), 12.

7   George S. Brooks, ed., *James Durand: An Able Seaman of 1812* (New Haven, CT: Yale University Press, 1926), 47.

8   Donald R. Hickey, *The War of 1812: A Forgotten Conflict* (Urbana, IL: University of Illinois Press, 1965), 20.

9   John Sugden, *Tecumseh: A Life* (New York: Henry Holt and Company, 1998), 188.

10 Harry L. Coles, *The War of 1812* (Chicago: University of Chicago Press, 1965), 18.

10 Hickey, 34.

10 Ibid.

11 Allan S. Everest, *The War of 1812 in the Champlain Valley* (Syracuse, NY: Syracuse University Press, 1981), 50.

12 John Spencer Bassett, ed., *The Correspondence of Andrew Jackson,* vol. 1 (Washington, D.C.: Carnegie Institution of Washington, 1926), 220–223.

12 David S. Heidler and Jeanne T. Heidler, "Madison's War Message, June 1, 1812," in *Encyclopedia of the War of 1812*, 583 (Santa Barbara, CA: ABC-CLIO, 1997).

13 Hickey, 73.

13 Ibid.

14 Pierre Berton, *The Invasion of Canada, 1812–1813* (Boston: Little, Brown and Co., 1980), 91.

15 Ibid., 129.

20 Department of the Navy, "USS *Constitution*: Engagement with HMS *Guerrière*," *Naval Historical Center,* October 25, 1999, <http://www.history.navy.mil/docs/war1812/const5.htm> (October 2, 2003).

20 Hickey, 94.

20 Henry Adams, *The War of 1812,* ed. Major H. A. DeWeerd (1944; repr., New York: Cooper Square Press, 1999), 28.

20 Berton, *Invasion,* 226–227.

21 Ibid., 233.

21 Adams, 43.

22 Samuel Leech, "HMS *Macedonian* vs. USS *United States,* 1812," in *Every Man Will Do His Duty: An Anthology of Firsthand Accounts from the Age of Nelson,* ed. Dean King and John B. Hattendorf, 308 (New York: Henry Holt and Co., 1997).

23 Donald Graves, "Songs of the War of 1812," *The War of 1812 Website,* n.d., <http://www.warof1812.ca/songs.htm> (October 9, 2003).

25 Adams, 57.

25 Hickey, 86.

28 John K. Mahon, *The War of 1812* (Gainsville, FL: University of Florida Press, 1972), 141–142.

30 Sugden, 337.

31 Hickey, 130.

31 Adams, 89.

33 Hickey, 156.

35 Benson J. Lossing, *The Pictorial Field-Book of the War of 1812* (New York: Harper & Brothers, 1869), 531.

35 Hickey, 133.

36 Jesse S. Myer, *Life and Letters of Dr. William Beaumont* (St. Louis: C.V. Mosby Co., 1912), 50.

36 William G. Rothstein, *American Physicians in the Nineteenth Century* (Baltimore: The Johns Hopkins University Press, 1972), 49.

36 Hickey, 129.

37 Sudgen, 360.

41 Hickey, 151.

42 Pierre Berton, *Flames across the Border, 1813–1814* (Toronto: Random House, Canada, 1981), 324.

43 Hickey, 187.

44 Nathan Miller, *Broadsides: The Age of Fighting Sail* (New York: John Wiley & Sons, 2000), 338.

45 Joseph T. Wilson, *The Black Phalanx: African American Soldiers in the War of Independence, the War of 1812, and the Civil War* (1890; repr.: New York: Da Capo Press, 1994), 79.

45 Robert V. Remini, *The Battle of New Orleans* (New York: Viking Penguin, 1999), 38.

47 Berton, *Flames,* 336.

47 Adams, 186.

48 Richard V. Barbuto, *Niagara 1814: America Invades Canada* (Lawrence, KS: University Press of Kansas, 2000), 252.

51 Kate Caffrey, *The Twilight's Last Gleaming: Britain vs. America, 1812–1815* (New York: Stein and Day, 1977), 238.

52 Anthony S. Pitch, *The Burning of Washington: The British Invasion of 1814* (Annapolis, MD: Naval Institute Press, 1998), 87.

53 Adams, 227.

55 Everest, 164.

57 Ibid., 185.

58 Lossing, 870.

58 Caffrey, 257.

62 Hickey, 209.

64 S. F. Wise and Robert Craig Brown, *Canada Views the United States: Nineteenth-Century Political Attitudes* (Toronto: Macmillan of Canada, 1967), 28.

64 Caffrey, 225.

64 J. Mackay Hitsman, *The Incredible War of 1812: A Military History* (Toronto: University of Toronto Press, 1965), 206.

65 Remini, 85–86.

66 Coles, 225.

67 Hickey, 211.

67 Ibid., 212.

67 Ibid., 299.

SELECTED BIBLIOGRAPHY, FURTHER READING, AND WEBSITES

SELECTED BIBLIOGRAPHY

Adams, Henry. *The War of 1812.* Edited by Major H. A. DeWeerd. 1944. Reprint, New York: Cooper Square Press, 1999.

Barbuto, Richard V. *Niagara 1814: America Invades Canada.* Lawrence, KS: University Press of Kansas, 2000.

Berton, Pierre. *Flames across the Border, 1813–1814.* Toronto: Random House, Canada, 1981.

_____. *The Invasion of Canada, 1812–1813.* Boston: Little, Brown and Co., 1980.

Caffrey, Kate. *The Twilight's Last Gleaming: Britain vs. America, 1812–1815.* New York: Stein and Day, 1977.

Coles, Harry L. *The War of 1812.* Chicago: University of Chicago Press, 1965.

Engelman, Fred L. *The Peace of Christmas Eve.* New York: Harcourt Brace & World, 1960.

Everest, Allan S. *The War of 1812 in the Champlain Valley.* Syracuse, NY: Syracuse University Press, 1981.

Horsman, Reginald. *The War of 1812.* New York: Alfred A. Knopf, 1969.

Lossing, Benson J. *The Pictorial Field-Book of the War of 1812.* New York: Harper & Brothers, 1869.

Mahon, John K. *The War of 1812.* Gainesville, FL: University of Florida Press, 1972.

Pitch, Anthony S. *The Burning of Washington: The British Invasion of 1814.* Annapolis, MD: Naval Institute Press, 1998.

Remini, Robert V. *The Battle of New Orleans.* New York: Viking Penguin, 1999.

Roosevelt, Theodore. *The Naval War of 1812.* 1882. Reprint, New York: Modern Library, 1999.

Sugden, John. *Tecumseh: A Life.* New York: Henry Holt and Company, 1998.

Suthren, Victor. *The War of 1812.* Toronto: M&S, 1999.

SUGGESTED FURTHER READING

Alder, Elizabeth. *Crossing the Panther's Path.* New York: Farrar Straus & Giroux, 2002.

Aller, Susan Biven. *Tecumseh.* Minneapolis: Lerner Publications Company, 2004.

Behrman, Carol H. *Andrew Jackson.* Minneapolis: Lerner Publications Company, 2003.

Bohannon, Lisa Frederiksen. *The American Revolution.* Minneapolis: Lerner Publications Company, 2004.

Cwiklik, Robert. *Tecumseh, Shawnee Rebel.* New York: Chelsea House, 1993.

Lawson, John. *If Pigs Could Fly.* Boston: Houghton Mifflin, 1989.

Mitchell, Barbara. *Father of the Constitution: A Story about James Madison.* Minneapolis: Lerner Publications Company, 2004.

Patrick, Jean L. S. *Dolley Madison.* Minneapolis: Lerner Publications Company, 2002.

Roberts, Jeremy. *James Madison.* Minneapolis: Lerner Publications Company, 2004.

Robinet, Hariette Gillem. *Washington City Is Burning.* New York: Atheneum, 1996.

Weitzman, David. *Old Ironsides, Americans Build a Fighting Ship.* Boston: Houghton Mifflin Company, 1997.

Whelan, Gloria. *Once on This Island.* New York: HarperCollins, 1995.

Young, Robert. *A Personal Tour of Old Ironsides.* Minneapolis: Lerner Publications Company, 2001.

WEBSITES

An American Hero: Tecumseh
<http://www.jmu.edu/madison/tecumseh>

The Battle of Lake Erie
Niagara History
<http://www.brigniagara.org/battle.htm>

The Battle of New Orleans
The Cabildo Museum
<http://lsm.crt.state.la.us/cabildo/cab6.htm>

The Battle of Plattsburgh
The Battle of Plattsburgh Association
<http:/www.battleofplattsburgh.org>

Dolley Madison's Letter about the Burning of Washington
<http://www.nationalcenter.org/Washington Burning1814.html>

Fort McHenry
National Park Service
<http://www.nps.gov/fomc/>

The Star-Spangled Banner: The Story of the Flag
Smithsonian Institution, National Museum of American History
<http://wwamericanhistory.si.edu/ssb>

The War of 1812 on Lake Champlain
Historic Lakes Association
<http://www.historiclakes.org/contents.htm#1812>

INDEX

ABOUT THE AUTHOR

Diana Childress has published two books for young readers, *Prehistoric People of North America* and *Chaucer's England*, and more than fifty articles on history, archaeology, art, and science in children's magazines. She has a PhD in English literature from the University of Pittsburgh and taught college students for ten years before devoting her time to raising two daughters and writing. She has also worked as a school librarian and has written for social studies textbooks. A native of Texas, she grew up in Mexico and lives in New York City.

PHOTO ACKNOWLEDGMENTS

The images in this book are used with the permission of: Peter Newark's American Pictures, pp. 4–5, 18 (top), 21, 29, 32, 33, 40, 45, 74 (bottom); The Mariners' Museum, Newport News, VA, pp. 6, 24, 28; Walker Art Center, T. B. Walker Collection, p. 7; © Hulton|Archive by Getty Images, pp. 8, 39, 52; © Bettmann/CORBIS, pp. 9, 30; Ohio Historical Society, p. 11 (top); Library of Congress, pp. 11 bottom (LC-USZ62-106865), 13 (D4-8837), 14 (LC-USZ62-070643), 23 (LC-USZ62-7659), 27 (LC-USZC4-6223), 49 (LC-USZ62-1804), 58 (USZ62-27679), 60; National Park Service, pp. 16 (top, middle), 36 (left); © Brown Brothers, pp. 16 (bottom), 42, 74 (third from top); Chicago Historical Society, p. 18 bottom (DN-0001289); U.S. Naval Institute Photo Archive, pp. 19, 22, 35; © North Wind Pictures, pp. 26 (top), 37, 46, 50 (left), 57, 65, 74 (top); Peter Newark's Military Pictures, pp. 26 (bottom), 62; Museum of the City of Mobile, AL, p. 34; Courtesy of the Bakken Museum Department of Special Collections, p. 36 (right); National Archives, pp. 43 (NWDNS-111-SC-96967), 53 (NWDNS-111-SC-96969), 61 (NWDNS-111-SC-96970), 66 (NWDNS-111-SC-90818), 68–69 (NWDNS-111-SC-96965); Stock Montage, pp. 44 (top), 54; Courtesy of the New York Historical Society, New York City, p. 44 (bottom); Independent Picture Service, pp. 50 (right), 74 (second from top), 74 (second from bottom); National Gallery of Art, Washington, D.C., p. 55; Courtesy the Chicago Historical Society, p. 59; Virginia Historical Society, Richmond, VA, p. 75 (top); U.S. Signal Corps, National Archives Brady Collection, p. 75 second from top (111-B-4188); National Archives of Canada/C124, p. 75 (bottom). Maps by Laura Westlund, pp. 14, 40, 51, 63, 71.

Cover by © Francis G. Mayer/CORBIS